Working in the Police Force

Tony Judge

Batsford Academic and Educational   London

© Tony Judge 1985
First published 1985

All rights reserved. No part of this publication
may be reproduced, in any form or by any means,
without permission from the Publisher.

Typeset by JMP Typesetting
and printed in Great Britain by
Anchor/Brendon, Tiptree, Essex
for the publishers
Batsford Academic and Educational
an imprint of B T Batsford Ltd
4 Fitzhardinge Street
London W1H 0AH

British Library Cataloguing in Publication Data
Judge, Tony
   Working in the police force.——(Careers series)
   1. Police——Vocational guidance——Great Britain
   I. Title   II. Series
   363.2′023′41   HV8195.A2

ISBN 0 7134 2341 2

Contents

Acknowledgment 6

Captions to photographs between pages 64 and 65 7

Introduction 9

What is police work about? 15
Qualities required of a police officer 15
Social and family life 18
Am I the right kind of person? 19
Police Discipline Code 20
Pay 21
Housing 21
Pension scheme 22

How the police service works 23
Qualifications for police recruits 27

The first two years 29
Initial training course 30
Local procedure course 31
Attachments 31
Tutor Constable attachment 31
Progress and monitoring training 33
Community and race relations training 34

Promotion in the police service 39
Bramshill Police Staff College 41

All in a day's work 43
Crime 32
   Keeping within the Law 44
   Qualities of a good detective 46
   The growth of organised crime 48
   Murder cases 49
   Regional crime squads 49

All in a day's work — *continued*
   The Special Branch   51
   Forensic science   51
   Personal integrity 51
   Crime prevention   53
Traffic   54
   Driving skills   55
   Specialist squads   55
   Traffic and crime   56

The uniformed policeman   57
Career prospects   58
The peace-keeping role   59
Boredom   60
Qualities needed to be a good beat patrol constable   60
The value of experience   61
The beat officer   63
Community policing   65

Women police   69
The Sex Discrimination Act   71
Dealing with women and children   72
Dealing with violence   73
Qualities needed to become a policewoman   74
The Policy Studies Institute Report   76

Leadership   78
The Police Constable   78
The ranking system   79
Duties and responsibilities   79
The men at the top   99
   Commissioner of the Metropolitan Police   100
   Chief Constables   100

Police powers   106
The Police and Criminal Evidence Act   107
The Royal Commission on Criminal Procedure   108
The Police and Criminal Evidence Bill   111
Police discipline   113
Police accountability   114

Other police units   120
The Dog Section   120
Underwater Search Units   121
Mountain Rescue Teams   121
Police Horses   122
River Police   122
Police Helicopter Units   123

The 'other' forces   124
British Transport Police   124
Ministry of Defence Police   124
Royal Park Police   124
Docks Police   125
Atomic Energy Authority   125
The Armed Services   125

Civilians in the police   127
Scenes of Crimes Officers   128
    Fingerprints   128
Police photographers   129
Computer Operators   130
Police Operations   130
Traffic Wardens   130

Special Constables   132

Facing the future   134

Index   139

ACKNOWLEDGEMENT

I am grateful to many friends in the police service for their help and advice during the writing of these chapters. My wife, Jean, was extremely patient when writing the book had to take priority over family matters and Joan Robson helped a lot in a variety of ways. Lastly, I must thank Thelma Nye of Batsford's for her forbearance, belief, and enthusiasm.

Surbiton
1985

Captions to photographs facing pages 64 and 65

1   A chief constable inspects police cadets at a Passing Out Parade at the end of their training course. *Nottinghamshire Constabulary*

2   Huge public gatherings involve major police operations. Here an officer keeps a watchful eye on crowds attending a pop festival. *Chief Constable of Cheshire*

3   A cadet helps a police photographer to photograph tyre impressions found at the scene of a crime. Sometimes a plaster cast will be taken to be used as evidence in court. *Hampshire Constabulary*

4   A civilian scenes of crimes officer checks for fingerprints at the scene of a robbery. *Northumbria Police*

5   A police motorway control unit which assists the police to attend at the scene of an accident or to deal with crime. *Thames Valley Police*

6   Police traffic squads have these special accident unit vehicles which contain all the equipment necessary for police control at the scene of a serious accident. *Lancashire Constabulary*

7   Police motorcyclists are used for ordinary patrol work as well as special functions such as escorting very wide vehicles on public roads. *Gwent Constabulary*

8   The Metropolican Police owns its own Bell Helicopters which operate from the Helicopter Unit at Lippitts Hill. Other forces make use of these machines on hire.
    Photograph: David Oliver

9   A police cadet assists a member of the public at a police station. *Fife Constabulary*

10 A modern police operations room makes use of a wide range of sophisticated technology. *Leicester Constabulary*

11   Several forces have Mounted Police Departments. Besides looking very smart on ceremonial duties, horses are used with great effect to control large crowds such as at football matches. *Northumbria Police*

12   Police dog with handler checking the security of a lock-up premises. *Gwent Constabulary*

13   Cadet with young officer learning about the beat. *Metropolitan Police*

14   Besides the Thames Division of the Metropolitan Police, forces with large stretches of waterways or coastline use launches. Here a police launch belonging to the Devon and Cornwall Constabulary is seen passing the Royal Yacht 'Britannia'. *Devon and Cornwall Constabulary*

Introduction

I begin this book with a quotation from the Report of Lord Scarman, who conducted the Inquiry into the Brixton Riots of 1981.

'During the weekend of 10-12 April the British people watched with horror and incredulity an instant audio-visual presentation on their television sets of scenes of violence and disorder in their capital city, the like of which had not previously been seen in this century in Britain. In the centre of Brixton, a few hundred young people — most, but not all of them, black — attacked the police on the streets with stones, bricks, iron bars and petrol bombs, demonstrating to millions the fragile basis of the Queen's Peace. The petrol bomb was now used for the first time on the streets of Britain (the idea, no doubt, copied from the disturbances in Northern Ireland). These young people, by their criminal behaviour — for such, whatever their grievances or frustrations, it was — brought about a temporary collapse of law and order in the centre of an inner suburb of London.

'The disturbances were at their worst on the Saturday evening. For some hours the police could do no more than contain them. When the police, heavily reinforced, eventually restored order in the afflicted area, the toll of human injury and damage to property was such that one observer described the scene as comparable with the aftermath of an air raid. Fortunately no one was killed, but on that Saturday evening 279 policemen were injured, 45 members of the public are known to have been injured (the number is almost certainly greater), a large number of police and other vehicles were damaged or destroyed (some by fire), and 28 buildings were damaged or destroyed by fire. Further, the commitment of all available police to the task of quelling the riot and dispersing the rioters provided the opportunity, which many siezed, of widespread looting in the shopping centre of Brixton.'

Introduction

This graphic description of the dramatic and frightening scenes at Brixton that weekend could apply with equal accuracy to the riots which occurred a few weeks later in the Toxteth district of Liverpool. There were similar but less serious disturbances in other cities and towns around this period, all involving groups of young people going on the rampage, often seeking out the police as the targets of their attack.

Nor were these the only outbreaks of widespread disorder which took place that summer of 1981. 'Mods' fought with 'Rockers' and 'Skins' with 'Punks' in many places. Seaside resorts experienced brief but bloody skirmishes involving gangs of several hundred youths at a time. Fairgrounds were often the scenes of pitched battles. It seemed as if a large part of Britain's younger generation had decided to declare war on authority, law and order, and especially the police.

At first, the police themselves gave the impression that they had been caught unprepared and they seemed unsure of what to do about mob violence on this scale. Fortunately this period of police uncertainty did not last for long. The police quickly developed new tactics. They stopped crouching behind riot shields and making themselves easy targets for the brick and petrol bomb throwers. Wearing fireproof overalls and tough helmets to protect their heads, they began to move in to break up gangs of troublemakers before they had the chance to mount the kind of sustained assault which had caused the police to sustain so many casualties. 'Snatch squads', modelled on the pattern used by the security forces in Northern Ireland, arrived in police vehicles and arrested ringleaders. The riots ended as quickly as they had begun.

The summer of 1981 may turn out to be a crucial turning point in police history. The lessons they had to learn were harsh. Here was a service which prided itself on being able, with general support from the public, to keep the Queen's Peace with a minimum of force. Before Brixton, there had been some ugly incidents, such as violent clashes at demonstrations and industrial disputes, but no serving officer could recall anything to compare with the fury and hatred vented against the police at Brixton and Toxteth. These young people did not support the police; they thought of the police as their enemies.

The first lesson for the police was that never again could they be caught totally unprepared to deal with a violent mob. As a result,

Introduction

all police officers likely to be engaged at any time in the future to deal with a street riot will have available to them proper protective clothing, helmets with face visors, flameproof clothing, reinforced boots, padding to protect vital body organs; lightweight smaller shields to give protection without sacrificing mobility. In reserve, and for use only in the last resort, police forces will have tear gas and even plastic bullets. If this makes the British police, when dealing with public disorder, look and act very much like the paramilitary police units of other countries, such as the much feared CRS in France, that is the sad but inevitable consequence of the summer of 1981.

The second lesson for the police was that they must rethink their training and tactics, and their arrangements for mobilising large scale reinforcements at short notice. Against all its previous traditions the British police service finds itself with a 'third force' to deal swiftly and effectively with mass disorder. In 1984, the lessons learned in 1981 were employed in the handling of the coal dispute.

There were other lessons which arose from the riots. These were not as capable of instant solution and decision. Lord Scarman put it succinctly:

'The policing problem is not difficult to identify: it is that of policing a multi-racial community in a deprived inner city area where unemployment, especially among young black people, is high and hopes are low. It is a problem which admits of no simple or clear cut solution. We require of the police that they maintain and enforce the rule of law in our ethnically diverse society. Without an appreciation of the needs and aspirations of the many elements which constitute that society it is impossible to set the standards for successful policing. Unless the police adjust their policies and operations so as to handle these difficulties with imagination as well as firmness, they will fail.'

Lord Scarman found that there was between the police in Brixton and the majority of the young black people in the area a huge gulf. There was bitter resentment of the tactics which the police had used to combat a wave of street crime — 'mugging', by putting large numbers of police on the streets to carry out searches. It was claimed that the police were racialists and that black people could expect to be brutalised in police stations and be the victims of false police evidence in the courts. Lord Scarman did not accept that there was widespread police racialism or that police misconduct

Introduction

was on anything like the scale suggested by some of the witnesses who gave evidence to him, but he confirmed that there were some abuses and that the gulf in understanding between young blacks and the police was very great. He made a number of suggestions, including the idea of better consultation between the police and local communities, and better training in race relations for the police.

The police have shown that they are willing to learn from the riots and they accept most of the ideas put forward by Lord Scarman, but three years after the riots there was still tension and suspicion of the police in the multi-racial areas of London. Here and in Toxteth voices were heard saying that little or nothing had been achieved and there was much speculation about the possibility of a repetition of the 1981 riots. Obviously, no matter how much the police try to restore public confidence in their role, it will take a long time for the bitterness and suspicion to be replaced by understanding and co-operation.

Of course, Britain is not just the troubled inner cities. There are many parts of the country where the police enjoy the full support of the people. Opinion polls show consistently that the police service stands high in public esteem. Yet there is no question that what was once total support from the vast majority of the population can no longer be taken for granted. Apart from the inner city tensions, the reputation of the police has suffered in recent years by the revelation of serious corruption in some parts of the Metropolitan Police. There has been growing public concern about the way in which complaints against the police are investigated, and whether the police are truly accountable for their actions. Added to this, there is anxiety about the big increases in reported crimes and the apparent inability of the police to bring more than a small proportion of criminals to justice.

Whilst all these issues have to be kept in perspective, because of the fact that there is still a big majority of the public who support and admire the police service, it is also a fact that police officers today have a much more difficult task than was the case, say, ten or twenty years ago. We live in an age when more people are conscious of their rights and ready to challenge authority. The police officer is out on the streets to uphold and, if necessary, enforce the Law. He has only limited powers to help him and any attempt on his part to exceed these powers puts him in the wrong. When faced with

Introduction

some difficult situations, the policeman has to rely on himself, his tact and common sense. He needs to have these qualities, perhaps to a greater extent than he would need them to carry out almost any other job.

When we think of the police we think first of their role as crime fighters, and most police operational policies and practices are directed towards the prevention and detection of crime. Yet the police have many other responsibilities. Far more people are killed and injured in traffic accidents than are ever the victims of criminal violence, so the protection of life on the roads is a paramount duty for the police. Then there is the social role of the police. Our society employs many different types of social workers, but so often the first place that the citizen turns to when he is confronted with an emergency is the local police station. It may be a case of a missing relative, or neighbours who are anxious about an old person living alone who has not been seen for some time. Then again it may be a case of suspected cruelty to a child. The police is the one social service which the public knows will be open and available all around the clock, every day of the year. One essential quality in the make-up of a good police officer is a willingness to be of help to his fellow citizens. The policeman who lacks that quality soon finds that he has joined the wrong job.

I have spent the last 30 years in everyday association with police officers. I am well aware of the fact that not every policeman is as good as he ought to be, and that a few fall well below the standards we expect of our police. Yet, whenever I hear someone complaining about the police, I am reminded of someone who was for many years my closest personal friend. He joined the same police force as I did and we first met at the recruit training centre. He was a carefree man with an infectious personality, always looking on the bright side of any situation. He was a natural athlete who was good enough to have been a professional soccer player or cricketer. When he married, I was the best man at the wedding. My friend was what is sometimes called 'a born policeman'. He had never wanted any other career, and he soon distinguished himself as a young constable with a number of smart arrests of people who had committed serious crimes. Naturally, he made progress in his career and in his early thirties he had reached the rank of superintendent and was confidently expected to go even higher.

One sunny Sunday morning, my friend was the officer in charge

Introduction

of the police station in a seaside town. Suddenly, a message was received that a gang of armed men had tried to rob a shop in the town centre, and that shots had been fired at the police who were pursuing the criminals in a car chase. My friend, accompanied by an inspector, immediately left his office and joined in the chase. Over the car radio they heard that two other officers had been shot and wounded by the robbers. Within a few minutes, they saw the robbers' car and gave chase. When the other car was driven into a cul de sac, the robbers abandoned it and made off on foot. My friend and the inspector followed one of them and cornered him against a wall. He turned and threatened them with the gun. Without hesitating, my friend grappled with the man and tried to disarm him. The man pressed the gun against the policeman's body and fired. Despite a frantic ambulance dash to hospital and the efforts of the surgeons, the wound was a fatal one and he died later that day.

My friend had played a big part in the life of that town. I knew that he was a popular figure, but I will never forget the huge crowds that attended the funeral service and the feelings of shock and grief that were so evident. Those citizens knew that they had lost a fine police officer and a good friend. He died because he was first and foremost a police officer, sworn to uphold the Law, and because he was also a leader and knew that the only way to lead is from the front.

My friend's name is Gerald Richardson, and it is to him that this book is respectfully dedicated, in the hope that some of those who care to read it, and afterwards become police officers, will prove themselves worthy successors of the thousands of police officers who are just as he was.

What is police work about?

Ever since the first fully professional police force in Britain, the Metropolitan Police, was founded in 1829, police officers have had two major tasks to perform. They must protect the life and property of the citizen, and they must prevent and detect crime. Those are the 'primary objects' of the police service and today they still govern the way in which our police forces are organised, and how they operate.

The young person who is fortunate enough to be accepted into the modern police service is embarking upon a unique career. The job of a police officer is unlike any other. On the credit side, it offers great variety and interest, job satisfaction, and the opportunity for advancement. On the debit side, it imposes heavy personal responsibilities and makes constant demands on the individual. This is not the kind of job which begins with the start of each working day and finishes at the end of it. Being a police officer means being so all the time. Policing is both a job and a way of life, as those who join the service discover very quickly. Therefore, someone who is thinking about the police as a career needs to think deeply and to find out as much as possible before making a decision to apply to join.

Finding out about what is involved in a police career is easy enough. There are pamphlets available from any police station which explain such things as the qualifications needed, physical requirements, rates of pay and so on. What is more important is to appreciate the nature of the job. Every prospective applicant should ask himself; 'Am I the kind of person who can do the things that a police officer has to do, and would I wish to do them?'

Qualities required of a police officer

A police officer, after all, is a special kind of person, and it is not everyone who would be able to accept the responsibilities he has to

What is police work about?

carry. Although most people still respect and even admire the police, these days they have far more critics than they used to have, and some sections of the population are now hostile towards them. It may be almost a hundred years since W. S. Gilbert wrote his famous comic song about 'a policeman's lot is not a happy one', but some of the things a police officer has to do can never be popular. Motorists, for example, hate being stopped by a police car and prosecuted for exceeding the speed limit. They think the police should pay attention to more important things, such as catching the real criminals, and leave respectable citizens alone. Many young people think that the laws on the possession of drugs such as cannabis are ridiculous, and they resent it when the police prosecute them for possessing small quantities of 'grass'. In inner city areas, there is widespread resentment of the police when they use their powers to stop young people on the streets and search them to see if they are carrying stolen property. All these matters will be discussed later on in this book, but they are mentioned now just to illustrate that many aspects of policing can be unpopular. Everyone likes to see a friendly British Bobby helping old ladies across the road or chatting to children, but that same familiar figure has other things to do which are not pleasant and lead to problems with the community. The police officer has to uphold the Law. It is the Government, through Parliament, which makes the Law, not the police. But it is the police officer who is criticised when a person objects to what a policeman does to uphold the Law. To that extent, what Gilbert wrote all those years ago is even more true today. There are indeed many times when 'a policeman's lot is not a happy one'.

One of the reasons why a police officer's job is nowadays more difficult than it was in the past, is that modern society has undergone major social changes in a comparatively short period of time. The policeman, perhaps more than any other public servant, represents authority, and today people will question authority where once it was taken more or less for granted. They are far more aware of their rights and will not stand for what they see as an abuse of authority by officials, including those officials in police uniforms. It is often said that, 'in the good old days', the policeman on his beat had absolute authority, 'the monarch of all he surveyed'. There is nostalgic talk of how the local policeman was a much respected figure who sometimes dealt out his own form of

What is police work about?

instant justice, such as 'a clip round the ear' of an erring boy caught misbehaving himself, and that such an action by a policeman was fully approved by the public. The modern policeman knows that he would soon be the subject of an official complaint and a thorough investigation if he resorted to such methods. One of the things he has to learn very quickly is how to establish his authority, when dealing with members of the public, without using physical violence or in any way exceeding the strict limitations which the Law places on his powers. For example, the Law allows a police officer to arrest a person, but he must have sound reasons for depriving a citizen of his liberty, and the Law lays down strict limitations on the powers of the police to keep citizens in custody, and on the ways in which police can question suspects.

The nature of a police officer's job is such that he spends a lot of his time preventing people from doing what they wish to do, whether it is a trivial thing such as riding a bicycle upon the footpath, or something far more serious, such as breaking into property. Of one thing he can be certain, the last thing a person is going to do, when a policeman takes such preventive action, is to thank him! Of course, there are many more occasions when a police officer is able to help members of the public and then he is regarded in a much more favourable way, but in his law enforcement role he can never expect to be popular all the time.

There is an old saying; 'A policeman does not have friends'. This is not literally true, but it reflects the fact that police officers are expected to show neither favour nor prejudice towards any members of the public. For this reason, a police officer has to be careful in his choice of friends. The service imposes certain restrictions on the private lives of police officers, all of which are designed to preserve his impartiality. This is something that tends to set the police officer apart from other citizens who are able to keep their working lives and their private lives separate from each other. The Police Regulations, which apply to all members of the police service, state that a constable shall at all times abstain from any activity which is likely to interfere with the impartial discharge of his duties. A police officer is not allowed to take on any other employment and he may not have an interest in a business unless he has the permission, which is rarely granted, of his chief officer. This prohibition on business activity applies to any member of a

What is police work about?

policeman's family who lives with him. A policeman may not take an active part in politics, although he is allowed to vote in elections. All these regulations are concerned with ensuring that a police officer does not do anything to interfere with his obligation to be impartial, but there are others which also restrict his private life in a way which does not apply to other people. The place where he lives must be approved as suitable for a police officer to occupy. He may not have a lodger in his home without the permission of his chief officer. It is a disciplinary offence for a police officer to fail to discharge a debt. A policeman must not place himself under any financial obligation to a member of the public. He is not even allowed to give a reference or a testimonial on behalf of a citizen unless he has received permission from his superior officer.

Social and family life

It is not simply these restrictive regulations which underline the difference between a police officer and his fellow citizens. The demands of the job interfere with the kind of normal social and family life which most other people are able to take for granted. To begin with, there is the problem of shift work around the clock and the frequent changes of duty which can occur, often without prior warning. It is quite common for a policeman to have to work on his rest day, especially in the busy urban police forces. A police officer is required to serve anywhere within the boundaries of his force and can be transferred at short notice. Sometimes this means that he and his family have to move home, with all the disruption that is involved in such a move.

There is no question that the demands of police work are felt by a policeman's family. A policeman's wife has special problems. In recent years, as violence towards the police has increased, police wives live with the anxiety of wondering whether or not their husbands will be the next to be assaulted. It is not unknown for the children of police officers to be bullied by other children simply because of their father's occupation, and they all experience the rather curious attitude of people who expect them to behave as model citizens, again because of what their fathers happen to be! And the police officer himself soon learns that he is never entirely 'off duty'. People who know what he does for a living will not allow him to forget that he is a police officer. Some policemen tend

What is police work about?

to resent this, because they feel that once their day's duty is over, they are entitled to enjoy themselves in just the same manner as anyone else would do.

These matters are mentioned here, not to put off someone who is considering the police as a career, but to point out that there are some drawbacks which have to be thought about. After all, a married man would have to consider, not only if he would be happy working as a police officer, but also whether his wife would accept the special demands of the job on family life.

Am I the right kind of person?

Let's go back to that original question; 'Am I the kind of person to do the things that a policeman has to do?' It is not everyone who will be able to arrest a criminal, or even to report a motorist for prosecution. It is certainly not everyone who can face up to a violent opponent, or help to quell a street riot in the face of bricks and petrol bombs. The sad truth is that police work in the last few years has become much more dangerous than ever it used to be. Every year, something like fifteen thousand police officers are assaulted in the course of their duties and some of them are seriously injured. There has been a steady annual increase in the number of incidents where criminals have used firearms to commit crime and the police have had to respond by training their members in the use of weapons, which are now carried by the police whenever they know they are likely to have to deal with armed criminals. Fortunately, the numbers of police officers who are actually killed by criminals in Britain remains very small, less than one officer a year during this century. In Northern Ireland, which is part of the United Kingdom, the picture is very different. No fewer than one hundred and fifty regular or part-time police officers have been murdered by terrorists since the present emergency in Ulster began in 1969 and hundreds more have been injured, some of them maimed or crippled for life. Over the same period there has been an increase of terrorism on the British mainland, where good police work has managed to prevent the terrorists being as successful as they have been in Northern Ireland. Nevertheless, terrorism has added a serious new dimension to modern policing.

The prospective police officer who is sure in his own mind that he could undertake the duties of a modern police officer next needs to

What is police work about?

ask himself why he wishes to be a policeman. There are many good reasons which point a young person in the direction of a police career; a wish to be of service to the community; an interest in the problems of crime; a belief in the importance of the rule of law, and so on. Quite the wrong reason would be a desire for personal power and a wish to push other people around. The police officer soon learns that he is the servant of the public, not its master. Some present day critics allege that some police officers abuse their authority and harass ordinary citizens, particularly if they are young and black. It is said that some police officers are racialists, or that they have unhealthy authoritarian attitudes and an arrogant attitude towards the public. When Lord Justice Scarman conducted an inquiry into the causes of the Brixton riots in 1981, he heard this kind of thing said by many of the witnesses who gave evidence to him. Some of Lord Scarman's recommendations dealt with this subject and the police forces themselves are well aware of the dangers of recruiting people with undesirable tendencies, such as racial prejudice or excessive authoritarianism. Whilst it is not always possible to detect such attitudes before a candidate is accepted, it needs to be stressed, despite what critics may say, that senior officers do not hesitate to deal with unsuitable officers whose conduct is likely to bring discredit on the reputation of the police service. This is one of the main reasons for requiring that all recruits serve for their first two years on probation. They can be dismissed at any time during this period if it is felt that they are unlikely to become efficient police officers.

Police Discipline Code

One other point that should be borne in mind when considering the police as a career is that this is a disciplined service. All occupations have some rules of conduct and many have disciplinary procedures for dealing with employees who do not perform their jobs properly; but few jobs place such emphasis on formal discipline as does the police service. There is a very detailed code of conduct called the Police Discipline Code and the procedures are laid down by the Police Discipline Regulations, which have been approved by Parliament. The Discipline Code deals with matters arising within the police force, and also with relations between the police and the public. In recent years there has been a great deal of public

What is police work about?

discussion about the procedures for dealing with complaints. All complaints are investigated in accordance with the requirements of the Police and Criminal Evidence Act 1984.

The Police Discipline Code sets out all the offences which a police officer might commit, such as discreditable conduct, which is defined as conduct which is reasonably likely to bring discredit on the service. As with many other matters dealt with in the Code, a police officer can infringe this section even when he is off duty and not acting as a police officer. It is an offence for a police officer to fail to carry out any lawful order which is given to him by a superior, or to fail to report any matter which it is his duty to report. He also commits an offence if he makes any false statement, or breaches confidence by disclosing information outside the police force.

The existence of the Discipline Code and the formal disciplinary procedures, under which a police officer who commits an offence may be punished in a variety of ways, including dismissal, serve to emphasise that the service maintains very high and exacting standards of personal conduct. It cannot be otherwise in a service which must rely upon the integrity of its members. Some people would find the disciplinary requirements of the service irksome, but in practice police discipline is very much a matter of common sense and self discipline and the vast majority of officers never find themselves in any difficulty of this kind.

Pay

There are many positive aspects to be considered when thinking about a police career. In the past, police pay has not been one of the major attractions, but more recently the police officer has been paid a good salary. A special committee was set up by the Government in 1977, under Lord Justice Edmund Davies and this recommended new rates of pay which were accepted by the Government and have since been kept up to date by annual reviews. There is no point in setting out precise rates of pay here because they change each year but details can be obtained from police stations.

Housing

A major financial benefit enjoyed by police officers is the provision

What is police work about?

of housing free of rent and rates, or the payment of an allowance, called a rent allowance, in lieu of police accommodation. This allowance has enabled most married police officers to buy their own homes, although some forces do not permit officers to become owner occupiers until they have completed several years' service. The rent allowance is fixed locally by each force and the amount a member receives depends upon the house he owns. Single police officers either live in free quarters or receive a flat rate allowance which equals half the maximum rent allowance paid to married officers. Single officers with more than five years' service who are aged over 30 can receive a rent allowance in the same way as married officers. *(The system was under review in 1984.)*

Pension Scheme

The police also enjoy another benefit in their pension scheme, which provides for retirement after 30 years' service on a pension of two thirds of their final pay. This means that most police officers retire much earlier than other workers. The scheme also provides for retirements due to ill health and there are special provisions for officers who are forced to retire after being injured on duty; for widows, and for the families of officers killed on duty.

The police forces tend to play down the financial aspects of the job when they publish recruiting literature, because it is hoped that people will be motivated to join the police out of a wish to be of service, rather than because they are looking for a well paid job and security, but it is just as well to know that nowadays the service offers generous rates of pay and good conditions of service.

The person who has thought about a police career and considered all that is involved in becoming a constable should certainly press on with his application. This is one of the most worthwhile jobs in the community. It expects a lot of its members, but it offers a great deal of satisfaction in return. The police tend to be a closely knit calling with strong bonds of comradeship between colleagues. Working with the police is much more than just another job. It is a fascinating and demanding vocation, offering a real challenge to a young person.

How the police service works

The police in Great Britain are organised into a number of separate police forces. Control of the police is a responsibility which is divided between the government and the local authorities. In England and Wales there are forty three separate police forces. The largest is the Metropolitan Police in London. Unlike all the other forces, the Metropolitan force is not under the control of a local police authority but is the direct responsibility of the Home Secretary. The Head of the Metropolitan Police is called the Commissioner of Police for the Metropolis. He is appointed by The Queen on the advice of the Home Secretary. The Metropolitan Police has jurisdiction over the whole of the Greater London Council area and extends into some parts of Surrey and Essex. The City of London has its own police force.

Outside London, the police forces of England and Wales consist of six Metropolitan forces; the West Midlands; Greater Manchester; Merseyside; West Yorkshire; South Yorkshire; and Tyne and Wear. These are controlled by police authorities which are administered by the Metropolitan county councils. The other forces are known as county police forces. Some, such as Bedfordshire and Wiltshire, look after just one county but there are several forces which police two or more counties, such as Thames Valley; Devon and Cornwall; West Mercia; and Avon and Somerset. These forces are controlled by 'combined' police authorities with representatives from each county council in the area. All the police authorities consist of two thirds county councillors and one third magistrates. The police authorities are responsible for the provision and upkeep of an adequate and efficient police force in their areas.

Roughly one half of the money needed to run a police force comes from the local rates and the remainder from central government. The Home Secretary is responsible to Parliament for all police matters. He has to ensure that police forces in England and Wales are adequate and that law and order is maintained. He

How the police service works

exercises his authority in a number of ways. The chief constable of a force is appointed by the police authority, but their choice requires the approval of the Home Secretary. The same applies to the posts of deputy and assistant chief constables. To ensure that each force is maintaining its efficiency, the Home Office has an Inspectorate. Her Majesty's Inspectors of Constabulary are all senior police officers who each look after a region consisting of several adjoining forces. They make regular visits to each force in their areas and submit reports on the forces to the Home Secretary. In exceptional cases the Home Secretary has the power to withhold the government grant without which local authorities would have to find all the money to administer their forces. He would only take this drastic step if he was satisfied that the force was not efficient or that there was something seriously wrong with its administration. Another of the Home Secretary's powers enables him to compel a police authority to remove a chief constable on the grounds of inefficiency. In practice, very few difficulties arise and the system of shared control of the police between local and central government works well.*

One of the advantages which comes from the system is that all police forces operate to the same standards of efficiency and are governed by the police regulations. The police benefit through common rates of pay, pensions and allowances.

The size of a police force varies according to the size of the area it polices, the population, and the nature of the demands made upon it. There is, for example, a much greater problem of crime in towns and cities than there is in the rural areas, so more police are needed in the towns. Only a few forces can be described as wholly rural, most have districts which are heavily populated. Some, such as Greater Manchester and the West Midlands, consist almost entirely of heavily populated areas. This is an important point to consider when deciding upon which force to join.

Each police force is commanded by a chief constable. In the past, many forces were under the command of chief constables who were not professional policemen, but former military or naval officers. This practice disappeared after the Second World War and

---

* In Scotland, the Secretary of State for Scotland is responsible for the police. The Royal Ulster Constabulary is answerable to the Secretary of State for Northern Ireland.

How the police service works

today every chief officer, including the Commissioner of the Metropolitan Police, began his police career as an ordinary police constable. In each force, there is a deputy chief constable who, amongst his other duties, takes charge of the force in the absence of the chief constable. He is also responsible for the discipline of the force. Next in line comes the assistant chief constable. It is normal to have an assistant chief constable in charge of each separate department of the force: police operations; crime; traffic; administration, etc. If the force is large enough to be divided into districts, it is usual to have an assistant chief constable in command of each district. The Metropolitan Police has a Deputy Commissioner and below him there are Assistant Commissioners in charge of the departments, assisted by Deputy Assistant Commissioners. Each of the districts in the force is controlled by an officer with the rank of Commander.

The precise way in which a police force is organised is a matter for the chief constable, so there are variations between forces. However, all forces have a separate Criminal Investigation Department and other specialist branches include traffic, crime prevention, training and community affairs, although in the latter case the titles differ and so may the nature of the work. All forces have police divisions, normally under the command of a chief superintendent. A number of divisions grouped together may form a district, as in the Metropolitan Police and other larger forces. Normally, a division would consist of not less than 200 police officers and of course most are much larger than this.

A police force division is likely to be divided into a sub-division, the larger of which would be commanded by a superintendent and the smaller ones would be under a chief inspector. Each sub-division is further divided into beat or patrol areas. Several beats may be linked together to be administered as a section of the sub-division.

Down to this basic level of section and beats, the organisation differs between forces. Usually, an inspector is in charge of a section in a rural police area but in the towns, where the constables are allocated to shifts, or 'reliefs' and operate on a 24 hours rota, each relief will be under the charge of an inspector with a sergeant to act as the constables' immediate supervisor.

It will be seen from the above that the command structure of the police service goes up from sergeant to chief constable, and each

How the police service works

rank has a higher level of responsibility than the one below it. However, this does not detract from the importance of the constable. Because the police service has a command structure, the public often thinks of the constable in the same way as it thinks of privates in the Army, but this is quite wrong.

Every police officer, no matter what rank he occupies in the force, holds the same office under the Crown; constable. It is this office which gives him his authority and imposes upon him his duties and responsibilities. The constable out on the streets of a city or patrolling a country district is there to uphold the Law. He is empowered to exercise his personal discretion in how he performs his duties, but equally he carries the personal responsibility and may be called to account for his actions in a Court of Law. It is a fact of police life that not every officer is going to be promoted, and indeed many officers choose to remain in the rank of constable. It is important to understand that it is possible to pursue a worthwhile career in the police service without necessarily seeking promotion, because the job of a constable can offer equal job satisfaction with that of an officer occupying a higher rank.

One choice which a prospective applicant to the police service has to make is that of the particular police force he would most like to join. A few years ago, this presented no great problem. Nearly every force was under strength and provided that the applicant fulfilled the physical and educational requirements and was considered suitable, he would probably be accepted. Recent developments have brought about a complete change in that position. First, there has been the big improvement in police pay, mentioned previously. This has resulted in most vacancies being filled and, because there are now very few cases of officers resigning before completing their term of service for pensions, the number of vacancies which are likely to arise each year has fallen sharply. Secondly, the unfortunate growth in unemployment in the country has made the police service a much more attractive proposition, especially because it offers job security. Therefore the opportunities for young people to join the police service in the near future have shrunk.

This is particularly true of one avenue of entry which used to offer youngsters the prospect of a police career straight from school. The police cadet schemes run by the separate forces used to provide between a third and a half of all recruit constables. Cadets could

How the police service works

join at any age from 16 onwards and expect to be accepted as constables when they reached the minimum age of 18 years and 9 months. Because so many forces are now virtually up to strength, there is no point in maintaining large cadet schemes if, at the end of the cadets' training, there is little chance of their being offered posts as constables. Some forces have stopped their cadet schemes altogether whilst all the others have cut back considerably on the number of cadets in training. Only the Metropolitan Police retains a cadet training scheme of any size.

Qualifications for police recruits

The Police Regulations, which are the rules made by Parliament to apply to every police force, lay down certain minimum standards and general conditions which candidates must meet before being acceptged for the police service. These are that the applicant must:

> produce satisfactory reference as to character;
>
> be aged not less than 18½ and, unless he has previous service as a member of a police force or by reason of other experience or his personal qualities is specially suitable for appointment, less than 30 (40 if he has previous whole-time service in the armed forces or as a seaman);
>
> be certified by a registered medical practitioner to be in good health, of sound constitution, and fitted both physically and mentally to perform the duties of a constable;
>
> be not less than 172cm (about 5ft 8in.) in height in the case of a man and not less than 162cm (about 5ft 4in.) in the case of a woman;
>
> satisfy the chief officer that he is sufficiently educated, by passing a written or oral examination;
>
> provide such information about his previous history, employment or other relevant matters as may be required.

In addition, candidates for appointment must be either British citizens, citizens of the Republic of Ireland, or Commonwealth citizens who have an unrestricted right to reside in the United Kingdom.

How the police service works

Chief officers can vary the minimum height requirements, and a number of forces currently have height requirements above the national minima. Conversely, chief officers may accept candidates who do not meet the minimum height requirements if they appear to possess other qualities or skills.

The most important consideration affecting a police force's decision to accept or reject a candidate is the character and calibre of the applicant. It goes without saying, surely, that persons with criminal records are not accepted. The only exception here might be in the case of a candidate who has committed an offence as a juvenile and has since lead a blameless life. The police make careful enquiries about the backgrounds of applicants. Besides people with criminal convictions, they are unlikely to accept those whose close relatives have been convicted of offences, or candidates who are known to associate with people of bad character.

The police are looking for persons who appear to have the necessary strength of character to undertake the very responsible job of a constable. A great deal will depend, therefore, on the way in which a candidate faces up to questions when he is interviewed by the recruiting board. Those making the decision will be looking for a clear indication that the candidate really wishes to make his career in the police, rather than just be looking for another job. They will want to know why he wishes to join the police. Is it simply because he wants to put on a police uniform and have authority over other citizens, or does he want to be of service to the community? It should be realised that on average the police only accept as suitable for appointment about one in six of all those who apply. At the present time, with a great number of candidates for the very few vacancies which exist, the police are able to be much more selective in their choice.

The choice of which police force to apply to is very much a personal matter for each candidate. Some will want to join their local forces to avoid having to move their homes on joining. Two points to be borne in mind are the type of policing likely to be encountered in the force; a predominantly rural force will not be able to offer the broad general experience of the larger urban forces, and the career opportunities which are likely to arise. In general, the young man who is anxious to make fairly rapid progress up the promotion ladder will find that the larger forces offer the best opportunities.

The first two years

The first two years of a police officer's career are very important for his future. This is called his probation period, because at any time during those two years he can be told that he is not likely to become an efficient police officer and his police career will be ended. Once his probation period is over, and his appointment as a constable has been confirmed by the chief officer of the force, then he cannot be dismissed from the service except after being found guilty of misconduct.

Although a policeman possesses all the authority and powers of a constable from the day he is first appointed to the force, it is obvious that he is only able to exercise these after he has been trained for his job. The probation period, therefore, is now regarded as a time when a young police officer is learning his trade. It is also a period when he is under almost constant and close supervision from his superior officers, who are watching to see if he possesses the qualities required of a police officer, and are ready to help and assist him with any problems he comes across. He is also very dependant upon the help and guidance which most of his more experienced fellow constables will give him, in order that he can cope with all the varied incidents which occur when he is on duty, patrolling his beat.

The system of training of police recruits and probationers has been thoroughly revised in the light of recent events. The 1981 riots in our inner cities came as a great shock to the police service, as well as to the general public. It had not been foreseen that a sudden outbreak of mob violence could overwhelm the police, who were supposed to be the guardians of law and order, and the guarantee against this kind of thing happening in Britain. Of course, there had to be changes in the system of crowd control and dealing with sudden outbreaks of disorder but, just as important for the police service, was the need to identify some of the underlying causes of the 1981 riots. In particular, the police needed to know to what extent they shared some responsibility for what had happened, and here the report of Lord Scarman was a valuable starting point for further enquiries. He looked very carefully at the existing training

The first two years

arrangements in the Metropolitan Police and he came to the conclusion that insufficient time and resources were being devoted to training young officers to cope with the very serious problems they would have to face on the streets of inner city areas. He recommended that a minimum of six months be spent on the initial training of recruits and that the training curriculum should be extended to provide training in the prevention, as well as the handling, of disorder, and in an understanding of the cultural backgrounds and the attitudes to be found in our equally diverse society.

Lord Scarman said in his Report:

> 'The period spent by a recruit on probation after the initial training course is an essential and integral part of the recruit training process. It should include practical training and supervision in the handling of people in situations of potential conflict such as stops in the street, training provided either through a "street duties course" or, preferably, through a tutor constable scheme. ... Probationer constables should not, save in an emergency, go out alone on foot patrol in an inner city or any other racially sensitive area.'

The swift response of the police service on the issues raised by Lord Scarman was to conduct a number of major inquiries into all aspects of recruit training. It is on the results of these inquiries that the current system of recruit training has been created.

The following explains what a police recruit can expect, in the way of training, from the time that he joins the police service until he completes his two years on probation.

Initial training course

In the Metropolitan Police, all recruits undergo a training course at the Metropolitan Police Training Centre at Hendon, which lasts for 20 weeks. Recruits to the other forces begin with a one week 'induction' course in their force and then go to one of the regional police training centres to undergo a course which lasts for 14 weeks, and is intended to give them a thorough grounding in the rudiments of a police officers' job. Of course, every policeman needs to know quite a lot about the law as it affects crime, traffic, and his general police duties. Something like a quarter of the content of the initial training course is taken up in lectures dealing with these subjects.

The first two years

Because physical fitness is so important for a police officer, a further quarter of the course will be occupied in physical education, drill and recreation. The police recruit will be taught about legal procedures, including the vital subject of how to give evidence in a court of law, and another large part of the course consists of practical demonstrations in which the recruit gets a chance to put into practice the powers he has been taught, in relation to crime, traffic and general duties. The remainder of the course is taken up in providing training on what are called 'associated police studies' and these include the understanding of cultural backgrounds and other issues involved in policing multi-racial societies.

Local procedure course

On his return to his home force from the regional training centre, the recruit undergoes a two weeks' local procedure course, which is designed to give him an understanding of how the force operates.

Attachments

Following the local procedure course, recruits can expect to be attached for brief periods of about two weeks to the force control room and to spend a similar period attached to an officer working a rural beat (in a county force) or a community beat in an urban force.

Tutor Constable attachment

As recommended by a Home Office report on police recruit training, all recruits in provincial forces can expect to spend about ten weeks on duty in the company of an older and more experienced constable, who is known as a 'Tutor Constable' and who has been specially selected and trained for this task. The idea of this system is, firstly, that young probationers just out of the training centres are not left alone on the streets, but also that the experienced Tutor Constable can pass on the 'tricks of the trade' which he has acquired during his years of practical experience.

In many respects, this is the crucial phase of the probation period. The training centre course can supply the police recruit with what he needs to know about the law and his powers as a constable,

The first two years

but it is only when he is out on the streets, dealing with real people and actual situations, rather than the artificial set piece demonstrations prepared by his class instructors at the centre, that the recruit comes face to face with reality. Before Scarman and the advent of the Tutor Constable system, the recruit came back to his force from the training centre and was literally thrown in at the deep end. The results varied from the successful to the disastrous, and many promising young officers brought their careers to an early end because they thought they were 'not cut out' for policing. For example, even a relatively minor incident like a domestic dispute between a husband and his wife, takes on far more tension and real problems when it is the real thing, and not a piece of play acting designed simply to test an officer's knowledge of his powers. Now, under the Tutor Constable, the recruit stands aside and watches, and hopefully, he learns. Of course, there is always the danger that he learns the *wrong* way, and this is why the police attach so much importance to picking the right kind of constables to be the tutors. They are all volunteers, but they have been chosen because they are known to their superior officers as reliable constables who can be trusted to work without the need for supervision, that they have the right attitude to their job and are not amongst the minority of disillusioned and disappointed constables who are, unfortunately, to be found in all forces.

It is at this stage, learning from a more experienced colleague, that a police recruit begins to understand (or at least he should begin to understand) that the real secret of successful beat policing is the proper use of discretion in the exercise of his powers. The sensible young officer soon learns that he does not have to arrest every person he comes across who happens to be drunk. Most drunken people are perfectly capable of finding their own way home, or are with friends who will look after them, and they are not making a nuisance of themselves or threatening violence to others. Yet there are some people who are drunk and quite incapable of looking after themselves who have to be arrested for the offence of being drunk and incapable, in their own interests. The policeman soon learns to distinguish between the late night reveller who has simply had too much to drink, and the unfortunate habitual and homeless drunk who would probably come to harm if he was left out alone at night in a severely intoxicated condition. Many such regular 'drunks' are in a condition

The first two years

bordering upon a coma; they drink large quantities of very cheap wine, often laced with methylated spirits or similar chemicals. Because they are physically in a very poor condition, their lives are at risk. There is very little the police officer can do. Society has neglected to provide treatment centres where rootless alcoholics can be weaned from their addiction, so they become one of the many problems which are left to the police and the prison system to deal with as best they can.

Especially in the inner city, multi-racial areas, it is hoped that the 'Tutor Constable' system will help to alleviate one of the major problems identified by Lord Scarman as being one of the factors which led to the riots. This is that very young and inexperienced officers had great difficulty in communicating with people, and this was particularly marked in the case of young white officers and young black people. Older officers, on the other hand, have learned how to establish a better relationship; their authority is less likely to be challenged, and they have learned by experience as to when a situation calls for firm police action and when tolerance and restraint are more likely to avoid trouble.

The present training arrangements are designed to keep the police recruit undergoing some form of training or continuous supervision until he has been in the police for at least seven and a half months. From this point onwards, he is deemed ready to venture out on the streets as a probationer constable who is equipped with sufficient professional knowledge, and has been trained to a point where he can reasonably be expected to cope with most ordinary situations, bearing in mind that he should be able to summon advice or assistance whenever it is required. For the rest of his probation period, however, he is going to be given more training, based on his initial course and intended to bring him to the standard which will be expected of him at the end of his probation.

Progress and monitoring training

In most forces, this takes the form of three further local courses, each consisting of two weeks. These courses are based on three main factors:
(1) those aspects of initial training which will profit from development when the officer has got some beat experience,

The first two years

and where his understanding has increased because he has been in contact with operational incidents
(2) the problems which probationers have to expect when they begin patrolling on their own
(3) the need to develop the probationer to the point where he can be regarded as (and he can regard himself as) a competent all rounder, who is aware of the make-up of the society in which he serves, and who aims as a police officer to make a personal contribution to the well being of that society.

Community and race relations training

This aspect of police work and training has become so important that it merits more detailed consideration in this part of the book, where we are discussing the young police officer at the outset of his career.

Let us be frank; over the past twenty years or so there has been a marked decline in the level of understanding between the police and large section of Britain's non-white communities. This is very much the case in relation to the young black and Asian people in our inner city areas. This resentment and hostility is said to have been the major cause of the Brixton riots and the outbreaks in other cities in 1981, but there have been many other examples of clashes between black people and the police.

It is very difficult to discover what exactly is the true situation. The police are often reluctant to discuss racism and prejudice amongst their own membership. But, just as it is unfair to categorize all police officers as racists, so it is ridiculous to suggest that all, or even the majority of, police officers, are not racially prejudiced and do not discriminate against black people. There are many reasons for the tensions which undoubtedly exist. On the police side, there is the knowledge that many young black youths take part in the committing of street crimes, such as 'mugging'. They indulge in soft drugs, such as marijuana smoking, because they see this as part of the West Indian, or at least the Rastafarian sect's, culture. Police officers, by the nature of their occupation, tend to resent nonconformists in society, and at present the largest and most visible group of those who do not conform to accepted standards of behaviour, conduct, and life styles, are the young blacks in the inner city areas.

The first two years

On the side of the young black people, there is the belief that police attitudes towards them are based on colour prejudice alone. It is alleged that young black people will be stopped and searched in the street, not because the police officer who stops them honestly believes that they may have committed or be about to commit, a crime (the only lawful reason for stopping and searching), but because they are black and dress in the West Indian fashion. There is a widespread belief that police, almost as a matter of routine, will arrest and charge black people without just cause and will invent false charges to justify such arrests; that they will assault black people in police stations; that the police will not protect black people from racialist attacks by white people; that they share, as police officers, the racial antagonism of the ultra-right wing groups, such as the National Front.

Given that both 'sides' to have developed entrenched attitudes over the years, and that there is a great deal of stereotyping, the efforts which the police are now making to eradicate racialism in their own ranks, deserve some consideration. In accordance with recommendations made by Lord Scarman, training in race and community relations is now an integral part of the police training curriculum. A Home Office Working Party on Community and Race Relations Training, reporting in 1983, recommended that community and race relations training should be designed to mix periods of formal training, to be undertaken in regional or force training schemes, with training on the job in a manner which will capitalize on the strengths of each. The initial training course at the regional centre now includes lectures which are aimed at laying the foundations for future training in this subject when the probationers have returned to their forces, whilst giving them a basic understanding of the problems they can expect to encounter when policing a multi-racial society. Part of the local force training now given to recruits emphasises this aspect of policing. Probationers also undergo training aimed at correcting wrong attitudes towards race and racial issues. This includes training in interpersonal and behaviourial skills, and in getting policemen actually to understand what is meant by racism. It has to be realised that it is possible for any citizen, not just a police officer, to have racialist attitudes without necessarily realising that they are such. Finally, the force training schemes now provide for further 'on the job' experience and formal training related to race relations

The first two years

problems. The Home Office Working Party which outlined the programme of race relations training which it considered to be necessary, proposed also that it was necessary for individual probationers to be assessed in relation to community and race relations when their fitness to be retained in the service on completion of their probation was being considered.

Some critics of the police role in relation to problems of race in Britain argue that training in this subject cannot eradicate racism in the police if young people who have racist attitudes are recruited. In 1983, for example, there was a major public outcry when a lecturer who taught academic subjects to youngsters at the Metropolitan Police cadet training establishment at Hendon, revealed on television the extreme racist sentiments which his students had expressed in some essays. The lecturer resigned from the Training Centre in protest because he alleged that the force was not concerned to eradicate such harmful attitudes, but his colleagues on the academic staff took a different view, and issued a lengthy statement in which they pointed out: 'These teenagers come to the Cadet School straight from school. For many of them, the Cadet School's multi-culture course is their first experience of anti-racist teaching.'

The Home Office Working Party also considered this question of whether it was possible to exclude anyone who had racist attitudes from the police service. They came to the conclusion that it was important to base race relations training on both attitudes and behaviour. Attitudinal training, they said, was important but would only be of value if it went together with the teaching of effective police skills. They added: 'It does not seem wise to rely entirely on the capacity of the "well trained" officer to mask his private attitudes. Our fear is that it is precisely under conditions of stress, and in circumstances where the benefits of adequate training are most needed, that unacceptable attitudes are likely to emerge.'

At this point, it is very relevant to discuss the question of whether or not young black people should join the police service. Many people argue that it is only when the number of black officers bears some relationship to the number of black people in the community, that the mutual suspicion between the police and the black communities will begin to break down. Others argue, from the opposite viewpoint, that black people should refuse to join the police because racism in the service is endemic, that the force

The first two years

merely tolerates black members in order to pose at being committed to multi-racial principles, and that black people who join the police are betraying the interests of their race.

It should be self evident that a 'black boycott' of the police service would undermine any chance of a permanent improvement in relationships between the police and black people. The young blacks who have joined the service have had to encounter some hostility and suspicion, but it has been from members of their own race more than from their colleagues in the police service. Young black people who are considering a police career, but are doubtful of the environment they will have to work in, could be well advised to go to the recruiting officers of the force they are thinking of joining, and discuss their fears frankly. Better still, they should be ready to approach black officers and ask them for their views. Of course, as in any other occupation, young blacks must expect to encounter the casual, somewhat unthinking and not over malicious racism which occurs in the workplace in many other occupations — ethnic jokes and so on. But it would be surprising if, from their own enquiries, young black people thinking about a police career did not find that the service's insistence on its commitment to a multi-racial police force is perfectly genuine. As for the hostility which black officers sometimes have to encounter, this is the reality which must be considered and weighed in the balance when making the decision as to whether or not to join.

The young black candidate for the police service will find that he is considered as a person, not as a member of an ethnic group. Although the police service is anxious to increase the representation of blacks in its ranks, there is a rigid policy of not lowering standards to accommodate any group. It is argued that there are sufficient young black and Asian youngsters who do match up to the physical and educational requirements of the service, not to give rise to a need to make special arrangements to accommodate other coloured applicants who do not fulfil minimum entry standards. However, some forces have taken to heart the idea, put forward by Scarman and others, that special additional training should be provided to help young black candidates to acquire the qualifications (which after all are not onerous by any comparable standards).

By the end of his first two years as a constable, the young officer should feel sufficiently self confident to tackle any situation. Once

The first two years
he is out of his probation, the support he has received in the form of constant supervision, regular training and assessment, falls away quite sharply. The police service has not fully developed in-service training for the more experienced officers, so often the post-probationer constable feels that he is being left to his own devices. Certainly, it is up to him whether he sees the completion of his probationary period as the point at which he stops learning about his job, and settles for the probability that he will remain a constable for the rest of his service, or whether he makes a conscious decision to be a career police office, anxious to broaden his experience by serving in the specialist department, to study for promotion, and to work his way up the promotion ladder. The police service is now sufficiently a profession to guarantee that advancement is purely on merit, and that for the able and ambitious officer the highest ranks of the service are always open.

Promotion in the police service

Every police force is commanded by a chief officer and senior officers who all started off as constables on ordinary duties. the principle of equality of opportunity governs the police promotion system and the way to the top is wide open for the officer who is determined to succeed. Apart from a small number of graduates who enter under a special scheme (and even they do not have an absolute guarantee of promotion) there are no special schemes which give one recruit an advantage over another. Some foreign police forces operate differently and allow highly educated people to join as 'commissioned officers' but the British police service does not. There was an attempt before the Second World War to establish an officer class through the Metropolitan Police College at Hendon. This offered selected constables and recruits from public schools and universities a short cut to inspector rank. The Trenchard scheme, so named after its founder, former Metropolitan Police Commissioner Lord Trenchard, was very controversial. It was disliked by the police and after the war, with the setting up of the National Police College, the Trenchard scheme was abandoned. There are still some voices to be heard in Parliament and elsewhere which argue that this insistence on total equality of promotion opportunities denies the police service its fair share of better educated people, but in recent years the number of recruits with good educational qualifications, including degrees, has increased greatly. This is due, of course, to the employment situation outside the service but for the time being, at least, the police are able to recruit their fair share of better educated recruits.

When discussing promotion in the police service, it should be appreciated that each post above the rank of constable has attached to it a supervisory function. The number of ranks above constable are strictly related to the size of the force, and to whether the post justifies a particular rank. This means that many people are bound to serve always as constables.

An essential requirement for promotion to sergeant, the first

Promotion in the police service

rung on the ladder, is to pass a three part examination in police duties. The examination can be taken at any time after a police officer has completed two years' service. Obviously, the sooner a constable takes and passes the examination the better, and the best time of all should be just after completing a period of probation when he has had intensive training. Yet the surprising truth is that there is a high failure rate in the examinations. This is in spite of the fact that all forces offer candidates the chance to study through local courses. The three papers in the examination deal with crime, traffic, and police procedure. If a candidate fails one of the papers, he has the opportunity of sitting that paper again in the following year.

No officer can be promoted to sergeant unless he has passed the examination and has completed two years' service. This minimum period of service can be a little misleading. In practice, only someone who has joined the police under the special Graduate Entry Scheme is likely to be promoted with under three years' service. This scheme provides for up to 24 graduates to be selected for appointment as constables in the police force of their choice. Provided that they complete their probation period satisfactorily, and pass the promotion examination, these graduate entrants are guaranteed a place on what is called the Special Course at the Police Staff College, and all officers who are selected for this course are promoted to the rank of sergeant as soon as they go to the College.

The Special Course is designed to produce leaders of the right calibre from within the police service. The idea is to find young officers of high potential. The standard expected is that a candidate for the Special Course should have, at the time that he is chosen for the course, the potential to rise fairly quickly to the rank of chief inspector. Besides the graduate entrants, the members of the Course are selected through a series of interviews. They spend twelve months at the Staff College on the Special Course. If they complete the Course successfully, they are promoted to the substantive rank of sergeant, and after 12 months' satisfactory service in this rank they are promoted to the rank of inspector, after which further progress depends entirely upon their performance. Such officers are 'on probation' in the rank of inspector for their first year in that rank. More information about the Police Staff College will be given later.

Promotion in the police service

Only a small proportion of the number of promotions to sergeant rank are concerned with the Special Course, about 60 a year. The great majority of sergeants are selected for promotion by force interview boards. It is unusual for a constable to be promoted to sergeant with less than four years' service. Officers who become sergeants at a comparatively early stage of their careers, say with less than ten years' service, are promoted on the basis that they are likely to be promoted again quite soon, in other words, they are regarded as career officers with ability and the ambition needed to rise high in the service. A small proportion of very senior constables is promoted to sergeant rank because it is felt that they can make the best contribution to the service at this level, normally as sergeants responsible for the supervision of constables.

The promotion system in the Metropolitan Police is unique to that force, because it has a competitive examination. Each year, there is a number of places available, based on the force's expectation of the number of vacancies likely to arise in the rank of sergeant in the following year, and candidates who reach the required pass mark at the competitive level are guaranteed promotion to the rank of sergeant. They must, however, before sitting the examination, obtain a certificate from their divisional chief superintendent to say that, in his opinion, they are suitable for promotion. The Metropolitan Police does retain a small proportion of the sergeants' vacancies for officers who have reached a minimum pass mark, but not the qualifying mark for promotion by competition. This ensures that some deserving senior constables, who may not be 'high flyers', receive some reward. These officers must have passed the examination, but at a lower level than the competitive examination requires.

A further examination is held for promotion to inspector from sergeant. This is open to sergeants who have completed two years' service in that rank. The ranks of sergeant and inspector are the only ones which require an examination qualification. Thereafter, promotion to higher rank is entirely by selection. All forces advertise vacancies for higher ranks and in this way many career minded officers apply for and obtain higher positions in other forces.

Bramshill Police Staff College

As we consider promotion in the police service to the higher ranks,

Promotion in the police service

the influence of the Police Staff College at Bramshill becomes clear. The College is the national centre of higher professional training for the police service of England, Wales and Northern Ireland. There is a separate college in Scotland although senior officers from Scottish forces, and from overseas, attend courses at Bramshill.

The eventual aim of higher police training is that all the highest ranks in the service will be filled by officers who, having joined the force as constables, will have progressed through basic training procedures as probationers, via the special and intermediate courses at the Police Staff College, through the Senior Command Course and, eventually, to top command posts as assistant chief constables in charge of major departments of police forces. On the way, many of these officers will also have had the opportunity of broadening their education by taking advantage of the scholarships offered to students on Bramshill courses, or through local force arrangements, which enable officers to study full time on degree courses at universities. Whilst the police service remains wedded to the principle that every police officer joins at the bottom of the promotion ladder, there is absolute equality of opportunity for the really bright, able, and ambitious police officer to reach the top.

All in a day's work

In general terms, the work of each police force can be broken down into three principle areas: Crime, Traffic, and General Police Duties.

Crime

The Criminal Investigation Department, as its name suggests, specialises in the investigation of crime, with the aim of detecting offenders and putting them before the courts. It is a mistake to think of the CID, however, as the department which deals with all crimes. By the early eighties, there were more than three million crimes being reported to the police in England and Wales every year. As a police force, on average, devotes only between 10 and 15 per cent of its total manpower to the CID, it is obvious that a large number of crimes have to be dealt with by members of the much larger uniform branch. The CID concentrate, in the main, on the more serious offences and those where there is some prospect of bringing the perpetrator of a crime to justice.

Perhaps the great majority of young officers join the force with the ambition of serving in the CID. It is regarded as the more glamorous part of policing, an image which has been fostered by detective stories, films and television programmes, few of which bear any relationship to the reality of working in the detective branch. Far from the heady and regular excitement depicted in a TV series, much of a detective's duty is made up of very routine work; visiting the scenes of crime, taking statements from victims, circulating descriptions of stolen property and suspects, checking criminal records; second hand property dealers and pawnbrokers (in search of the stolen goods) and asking for information from the small group of paid informers upon which a detective relies for so much of the information which comes to his knowledge. Detective work can also consist of long and weary hours spent on 'observations', watching the haunts of known criminals, keeping an eye on premises where it is expected that a crime may be committed. Still more time has to be spent on the tedious but

All in a day's work

essential work of preparing cases for court after an arrest has been made, taking statements from prisoners, witnesses and so on, discussing the evidence with prosecution lawyers, attending courts to give evidence and sometimes having to wait around for days on end until the court is ready to hear a case. Detective officers have to get used to working long and unsociable hours — criminal investigation can never be a 'nine to five' occupation. Whatever ideas an aspiring detective may have had at the outset about glamour and excitement, these soon give way to reality and the sheer hard grind of trying to cope with an ever increasing case load.

Yet there is something else which is always evident in the ranks of the detective department; enthusiasm. Detectives are dedicated officers who tend to become totally immersed in their work. They pride themselves on their knowledge of criminals and their ways, and on their ability to get results. Policemen are rather harsh judges of their colleagues, but they recognise and admire the qualities which go to make up a 'good thief taker', which is a much prized accolade in the service.

Keeping within the law

The experienced detective knows that he has to operate in strict accordance with clearly defined powers. Our system of criminal investigation and trial procedures is designed to ensure absolute fairness to persons who are suspected or charged with crime, and the balance is deliberately tilted in favour of the suspect, in order to minimise the risk of an innocent person being convicted of a crime. This insistence on police officers behaving strictly according to the law when investigating crime has recently been reinforced in codes of conduct which the Home Secretary has issued to all police forces. These codes are the legal requirements embodied in the Police and Criminal Evidence Act. They are designed to ensure absolute conformity to the legal rules when investigating crimes and dealing with suspects in police custody.

A police officer must have reasonable grounds for suspecting that a person has committed a crime (or is about to commit a crime) before, for example, stopping him on the street to question him as to his movements; or searching him for stolen property or offensive weapons. He has a general power of arrest for offences which carry sentences of imprisonment of at least five years and for a large

All in a day's work

number of other offences which are less serious but where it is sensible to empower the police to arrest the offender, for example, assaults. In all other cases, a police officer's powers of arrest are limited to cases where the offender's name cannot be otherwise ascertained or it is otherwise not practicable to deal with him by way of a summons.

The law makes it clear that a person who is detained by the police, either in the street or at the police station, has been arrested. No one can be 'detained for questioning'. The law also sets strict limits on the length of time for which a person can be detained at a police station without being charged with a criminal offence. A police officer who is investigating a crime is entitled to put any questions to any person he has reason to believe can assist him in solving that crime, but once he has made up his mind that a person he is questioning is, in fact, the person who committed the crime, then he must at once caution him, pointing out that he is going to be charged with a criminal offence and need not answer any further questions, and that whatever he says will be taken down in writing and may be given in evidence. This rule is designed to avoid allowing a suspect to incriminate himself. A person who is detained in a police station must be allowed access to a solicitor for legal advice, unless there is a very good reason to the contrary, such as the possibility that the inquiry might be jeopardised.

The existence of these and a large number of other rules, designed to protect suspects from unfair or improper pressures, can sometimes be regarded by the police as frustrating. There have been cases where it has been alleged that police officers have 'bent the rules' by making untrue allegations, such as that a suspect confessed to a crime whilst he was in custody. In court, the suspect has denied making any such confession, and it is alleged that here is another example of that notorious police practice of 'verballing' suspects, that is to say, the police officer has put incriminating words in the mouth of the suspect. To clear up any doubts about such matters, in which it is always difficult to establish where lies the truth because of the absence of independent witnesses of a conversation between a police officer and a suspect, it has been proposed that all interviews between police officers and suspects should be tape recorded. At present, extensive trials of recording equipment are taking place and it is probable that within the next few years, recording of interviews will be standard practice. It will

All in a day's work
be rather more difficult to devise a means of clearing up doubts about another malpractice which is frequently alleged against police officers, that of 'planting' suspects with incriminating evidence, such as stolen property or illegal drugs. At one time, the courts did not look very kindly on suspects or defence lawyers who made such allegations. It was said that the first action of a person who had no proper defence to a criminal charge was to attack the integrity of the police officers in the case. In recent years, unfortunately, there have been a number of proven cases of police misconduct of this kind which have resulted in the conviction of innocent people, and in some cases police officers have themselves been convicted of criminal offences arising from their behaviour in making investigations. These cases have shaken public confidence in police evidence. As a result, it has become easier to make allegations against the police and it is probable that more guilty men are being acquitted simply because juries in some cases have not felt it safe to accept the police evidence. This is, of course, a serious problem for the police and has served to emphasise the importance of good police practice in the investigation of crime.

Qualities of a good detective

The good detective, if he is to see his work brought to a successful conclusion by the conviction of the offender he knows to be guilty of a crime, must therefore work within this rigid and sometimes frustrating set of legal rules. His main weapon must be his own intelligence, coupled with his experience of criminals, and above all his skill in interrogating suspects. Detective work is specialised and requires additional training at one or other of the excellent detective training schools in the country, but such training tends to be aimed at improving the legal knowledge of detectives and explaining the aid they can receive from forensic science, and so on. Many detectives will argue that good detective work is a gift rather than something which can be taught, and that there is no substitute for practical experience in learning the craft of crime detection. Young police officers who have demonstrated an interest in crime and an aptitude for investigation during their early years, may apply to be considered for the Criminal Investigation Department. In most forces, those who are accepted are taken into the

All in a day's work

department on a temporary basis and then made detectives after attending an initial training course.

At one time, a Metropolitan police officer who was accepted for the CID remained in that department for the rest of his career. This is no longer the case and Metropolitan detectives are liable to be transferred to the uniformed branch, either on promotion or at the end of a lengthy period in the CID, for operational reasons. Similarly, officers who have been promoted in the uniformed branch may be posted to supervisory duties in the CID and *vice versa*. This system of interchange has always applied in provincial forces.

A detective soon learns that his success or failure as a thief taker depends on his own ability, coupled with the quality of the information upon which he is operating. Some of this comes from orthodox sources, such as through the criminal intelligence supplied by other members of the force who report on the activities of known criminals and their associates. Other assistance comes from the evidence of eye witnesses to crime, descriptions of stolen property, and clues obtained by the scenes of crimes officers who examine the locations of crime and obtain what scientific evidence there is to be had. But over and above these aids, the good detective needs informants. For the most part, these are people who are close to the criminal fraternity. They may often be active criminals themselves. They are prepared, almost always for money, to give a police officer particular information about crimes committed by others. Sometimes they will give information to revenge themselves on other criminals but the mainstay of the informant business remains money, with the added incentive that the criminal hopes and expects that 'his' detective will help him if ever he gets into trouble with the law.

Of course, operating in this way has its dangers for the police officer and for the interests of justice. There are strict rules governing the use and payment of informers. The police forces do not have large funds from which to pay informers; the rich rewards of betrayal come from the insurance companies who need to be satisfied that they are paying rewards in exchange for information which has led to the recovery of insured stolen property and, if possible, the arrest of the offenders. Whatever happens, the police must never encourage informers to 'set up' crimes by inciting other criminals to commit crimes, simply so that they can be arrested by the police.

All in a day's work
The growth of organised crime

The growth of organised crime in this country has been most marked in the past 20 years or so. Gangs of criminals get together to attack banks, post offices or security vehicles. They are invariably armed and they are prepared to use their weapons against anyone, police or civilians, who get in their way. The police have found that the most effective weapon at their disposal against this relatively new and extremely dangerous threat, has been the use of the 'supergrass', someone who has himself been involved in serious crimes but who wishes to avoid the lengthy prison sentence that must inevitably follow arrest and conviction. A supergrass will, therefore, be quite willing to give the police full details of crimes committed by other criminals and details of his accomplices. In return, he expects a reduced sentence when he is himself dealt with for the crimes to which he has confessed, and that the police will assist him to start a new life, often under an assumed name, away from the vengeance of the criminals he has betrayed. Whilst this method of entrapping major criminals has been very successful, and has enabled the police, particularly in London, to keep on top of the problem of serious organised crime, doubts are beginning to emerge about the supergrass method. There have been suggestions that some people have been convicted on the perjured evidence of supergrasses. The result has been that the courts are now much more suspicious of such evidence and the success rate has begun to decline. At the height of the system, major criminals were beginning to wonder whether organised crime, even with the huge rewards that can be obtained from a raid on a bank or a security vehicle, was worth the candle when they never knew whether the team of criminals with whom they operated, contained a potential supergrass.

The lesson for the police of the supergrass business has been, that whilst it is perfectly right for the police to take advantage of this ready demonstration of the fact that there is 'no honour amongst thieves', the value of wholesale betrayals of major criminals has been diminished by a readiness to take some supergrass evidence at face value, without looking for adequate corroboration with other supporting evidence, which would link the persons named by a supergrass to the crime alleged against them.

Organised crime is, for the detective, the 'cream' of his work. It

All in a day's work

is challenging and of obvious importance to the success of the police objectives of preventing and detecting crime.

Murder cases

Some other categories of crime are also regarded as of high value in detective work. Murder is an obvious example, but again the popular idea of murder mysteries solved by a piece of brilliant intuition by a detective, is very wide of the mark. The sad truth is that the vast majority of the five hundred or so cases of homicide which occur in England and Wales every year are 'family' killings, unpremeditated tragedies in which the victim is either related to, or very close to, the killer. This partly explains why the detection rate for homicides is so high, but the other reason, of course, is that the crime of murder is still regarded as the most serious of all, and each homicide which occurs will, unless the person responsible for the killing is known from the start, entail a major police operation. First, an incident room is established whilst a detailed scientific examination is made of the scene by forensic scientists, and a Home Office pathologist carries out a post mortem to determine the cause of death. Where there are no immediate suspects the police face a daunting task involving the statements of hundreds of potential witnesses, house to house enquiries, and so on. In some cases, it has been necessary to fingerprint thousands of suspects.

Some murder cases, such as the notorious Yorkshire Ripper, involve multiple murders carried out by the same person. The usual practice is to assemble teams of very experienced detectives from forces in the area, who pool their knowledge and the resources of their forces. Now, in the aftermath of the unfortunate errors revealed in the Ripper enquiry, the police are pursuing the idea of using computers to assist them in dealing with the massive problem of collating and evaluating the masses of information which pour in during a major and protracted criminal inquiry of this kind. Fortunately such serious cases are a small minority of total crimes.

Regional crime squad

The regional crime squads consist of experienced detectives, drawn from the detective departments of forces in the police region, who work together on the investigation of very serious crimes, keeping

All in a day's work

surveillance on known criminals in the region. Crime knows no boundaries, and criminals certainly are not respecters of police force maps. If detectives were concerned only with crimes committed in their force boundaries, they would have little knowledge of the highly mobile criminals who operate away from their home ground. The regional crime squads have been very successful in dealing with the problem of the itinerant major criminal.

Almost one third of known crime is connected with motor vehicles, and the theft of motor cars is a major headache for the police. The Metropolitan and other large forces now have specialist detectives working on this area of crime. Each year, for example, the Metropolitan Police Stolen Motor Vehicles Investigation Branch recovers stolen motor vehicles valued in total at around two million pounds. The criminal trade in high class motor vehicles, such as Rolls Royce cars, has international ramifications and involves the Branch in close co-operation with other countries.

Nowadays, international crime has spread because of air travel. The British police maintain an office of Interpol, the International Criminal Police Bureau, at Scotland Yard. The National Central Bureau for Interpol keeps British police forces in touch with Interpol offices in 130 member countries. Interpol as such (and contrary to the popular idea) does not investigate crimes, it acts as a clearing house for information and requests for assistance from the police in one country to another.

Unfortunately, international terrorism has added a new and dangerous dimension to the problems of policing Britain. London, in particular, has been singled out from time to time for the bombing activities of the IRA and other groups of terrorists. The Metropolitan Police CID is responsible for the Anti Terrorist Branch. Working closely with the Special Branch (see page 51), officers of this Branch concentrate on the movements of known terrorist suspects and gather information from people who are citizens of countries with known terrorist groups operating in Britain. The specialist knowledge they acquire of the personalities and complex politics involved in terrorism has been found of great value when serious terrorist attacks take place, such as the 1980 siege of the Iranian Embassy, or the case of the IRA terrorists in London's Balcombe Street siege some years ago.

All in a day's work

The Special Branch

The Special Branch is perhaps the least publicized branch of the Metropolitan Police (other forces maintain small offices staffed by detectives with similar duties and responsibilities). In the Metropolitan Police, about 400 detectives are employed in the Special Branch. Their major duties are to provide personal protection to British and foreign dignitaries. They also carry out enquiries on behalf of the Home Office concerning foreigners who are applying for naturalisation as British citizens. Members of the Branch also, through intelligence gathering, keep an eye on what are loosely described as 'subversive' activities, on the grounds that these could lead to breaches of the criminal law. This aspect of the work of the Special Branch is very sensitive and controversial. It is said that it brings the police perilously close to being political police, but the official answer is that the police are not concerned with the political views of those under surveillance, only with their alleged potential for breaking the criminal law.

Forensic science

As mentioned previously, forensic science nowadays plays an important role in the investigation of crime. Scenes of Crimes Officers, who examine the locations of crime to obtain scientific evidence, may be drawn from either the police or (and this is much more the case in the large forces) from civilian employees who have been recruited as Scenes of Crimes Officers. The actual scientific examination and analysis of such evidence is the job of scientists working in force laboratories or, in the more serious cases outside London, at the Home Office Forensic Science Laboratories.

Altogether, therefore, the criminal investigation department offers a varied and interesting range of work for the police officer who wishes to specialise in crime. The drawbacks of detective work are what they have always been — very long hours of work and the frustration of not getting results. It is a job which makes great demands on officers and family life tends to suffer as a result.

Personal integrity

Officers wanting a detective career should also understand that detectives must work on their own a great deal, or in pairs with a

All in a day's work

regular colleague, and are not as closely supervised as members of the uniformed branch. They are most vulnerable to allegations of corruption and misconduct. It is unfortunately the case that corruption is more likely to be discovered in the CID than in other parts of the police force, and this is because of the nature of the work. To be successful, a detective must cultivate the acquaintance of people who are criminals or their associates. There is a grey area involved in such associations and it is very easy for a detective to stray across the ill-defined line between what is permissible and what is likely to be regarded as corruption. For example, should a relationship which a detective has cultivated with an informer extend to bringing pressure on colleagues not to prosecute an informer for a crime he has committed? Should detectives socialise, when they are not on duty, with people of bad character? It boils down in the end to common sense and the officer's own standards of personal integrity. Some detectives, sadly, fall for the temptation of easy money in the form of bribes. The vast majority do not, but they have to expect to face accusations from criminals they have arrested. It has become fashionable to make allegations of corruption, as well as perjury and 'verballing', against detective officers.

One thing a detective has to learn to accept is the disappointment of losing a case in court. In theory, the police do not win or lose. They simply arrest the people they believe to be guilty and put before the court the evidence which supports that charge. What the court decides is a matter for the courts, not the police. That is fine in theory, but in practice it is a sickening blow to a dedicated police officer when he sees a case, which he may have spent weeks upon, collapse for no better reason than that the person charged had the benefit of a clever lawyer who was able to create doubt in the minds of the jury. But a detective must learn to live with such setbacks. What he must never do is go out of his way to make sure that a man he believes to be guilty is convicted, by manufacturing evidence to bolster what his police experience tells him is the weaker part of his case. This can take the form of 'verballing' or planting evidence, or using informants in ways which lead to allegations of entrapment, or getting other witnesses to give false evidence, and so on. A detective must learn that he is not employed by society to wreak revenge on the criminal. He may be angered by unfair attacks and sharp practice in the criminal courts, he may complain about the

All in a day's work

rules of evidence which most police officers believe are too much in favour of the criminal, but he must never betray his oath of office by demeaning himself to lie or bear false witness in other ways.

Crime prevention

Whilst the detective officer can be regarded as the 'crime specialist' in the police service, it has to be understood that every police officer is expected to be 'crime minded'. Crime prevention, after all, is regarded as better than crime detection, and one of the primary functions of a police force is to prevent crime from being committed. Here the value of the uniformed police officer, patrolling the streets of our towns and villages on foot, has always been recognised. It is also a fact that uniformed officers make more arrests for criminal offences than do their CID counterparts. This is due to two reasons; one the fairly obvious fact that there are far more uniformed police officers than there are detectives, and secondly, uniformed officers are far more likely to catch criminals in the act of committing a crime.

This is why police officers are trained and instructed to keep a watchful eye on the public. They learn how to detect the 'suspicious' person; to stop and question the stranger in the street, or to interrogate someone whose actions arouse their suspicions. This area of police work, as I have already mentioned, arouses a great deal of controversy and it is often alleged that the police use their powers to stop and search in order to harass young people, and particularly young coloured people. Used properly, the exercise of stop and search powers is an effective police weapon in the fight against crime, but police officers must remember that they are only entitled to use the power where they have sound reason for suspecting that the person being stopped and searched either has committed, or is about to commit, a crime.

A policeman who is 'crime minded' is said to develop a 'nose' for detecting criminals. It is a skill which owes as much to the personality, intelligence, and dedication of an officer who is said to possess these attributes, than to any mysterious secret powers. Success in this area of beat duty often boils down to keenness and an ability to get to know a neighbourhood and the people in it. Just as detectives rely heavily on their informers, so the successful beat officer relies for a lot of his 'criminal intelligence' on the willingness

All in a day's work

of members of the public to talk to him and to pass on information.

Dealing with crime is regarded, by the police and the public alike, as the major task of the service. Of late, there has been a great deal of public concern about the general performance of the police in coping with crime. The numbers of crimes reported each year to the police have been growing rapidly every year, from about half a million crimes a year after the war, to more than three million crimes a year in the eighties. And this is just the total number of crimes known to the police. It has been estimated that the true figure of crime may be many times more than the reported figure. Whatever the actual level of crime, it cannot be disputed that the police face major problems in trying to contain the level of lawbreaking in the country. The number of crimes recorded as 'cleared up' each year amounts to no more than about a third of all those reported. Fortunately, the police performance is much better when it comes to dealing with the kinds of crime which are regarded as the most dangerous to society (the overwhelming majority of reported crimes consist of thefts of property in which no violence has been used). The police have a good record in dealing with homicide (murder and manslaughter), crimes involving violence to individuals, and organised crimes such as bank raids.

Of one thing the police and the public can be certain; the problem of crime in our society is not going to lessen in the foreseeable future. All the indications are that the social problems which are said to give rise to crime are getting worse, and the need for a strong and effective police force, able to concentrate on crime prevention and detection, is going to be present all the time. And the success or failure of the police service is always judged by the general public, in terms of how efficient they are seen to be in the fight against crime.

Traffic

Inevitably, in such a highly developed society as our own, the police service finds a great deal of its time and effort occupied by the problems of maintaining the traffic laws and public safety on the roads. The police in the cities have the major problems. It has been estimated that, in the major towns of Britain, and especially in London, the volume of traffic wanting to use the roads at peak hours is about one third greater than the capacity of those roads to

All in a day's work

absorb such levels of vehicle movements. The inevitable result, of course, is traffic congestion, which is made worse when there is a conflict between traffic which wishes to move and traffic which wishes to park on the roads, for whatever reasons. Traffic congestion becomes serious when it is viewed in terms of delayed public transport, holding up of emergency vehicles such as fire engines and ambulances. Police forces work closely with local authorities in attempts to ensure that traffic management schemes, one way systems, waiting restrictions, traffic lights, and similar facilities, are all aimed at maintaining the flow of traffic.

Driving skills

Police officers who work in the traffic departments of police forces, driving police vehicles, attain a very high standard of skill as car drivers. They are taught how to handle their powerful vehicles at high speeds. As they are often called upon to answer emergency calls, their own lives and those of members of the public depend upon their ability to drive fast but with maximum safety.

Specialist squads

The motorway network of Britain, and our major trunk roads, require to be policed by specialist squads of police vehicles and drivers. These squads are adept at dealing with the sudden emergencies that arise on our main roads. Whilst motorways are generally considered to be the safest of all roads, the high speeds of vehicles using them invariably means that the accidents which do happen tend to involve serious injury and often deaths. The sombre side of such police duties lies in the task of tending to the injured and sorting out the terrible scenes of carnage to which police motorway drivers in particular, must become inured.

Specialist traffic officers need to be able to master the very complex motoring laws. There are literally hundreds of regulations governing the construction and use of motor vehicles and the laws controlling drivers, speed limits, vehicle licensing and insurance, are all matters with which specialist police officers working in traffic departments need to be familiar.

All in a day's work
Traffic and crime

It also has to be remembered that crime is inseparable from traffic. Many criminals use motor vehicles in the commission of crime, and police forces deploy their vehicles as much with crime as with traffic problems in mind. It is the highly skilled specialist police driver and his observer colleague who are so often at the scene of a crime, in answer to an emergency call, and able to effect the arrest of a criminal who has been disturbed in the act of committing his crime. This is one of the major reasons why the police service resists the frequent suggestions which are made for a separation of the police from their traffic responsibilities, with these being taken over by a separate specialist force.

The uniformed policeman

The most important part of the police service, and what is often called 'backbone', is the uniform patrol branch. It is a fact of police life that the great majority of the young men and women who join the service are destined to spend the whole of their careers (apart from attachment to other departments during training) as members of the uniformed branch. Many, of course, will remain in the branch as constables throughout their police careers. This will not always be from their own choice; some are never able to pass the promotion examinations and thus do not qualify for promotion. Although the promotion examinations each year do not produce many successful candidates (a failure rate of about three out of every four who enter, almost entirely due to the inability of candidates to prepare themselves properly for the examination), there are still many more qualified officers waiting for promotion than there are vacancies.

This situation is getting worse because of a number of reasons. The sixties and seventies were eras of rapid expansion and change in the police service. More police officers meant more promotion opportunities, and the growth of specialist departments created more supervisory posts. In recent years, this process has slowed considerably, and promotion opportunities now depend for the most part on the rate at which existing holders of the ranks above constable leave the service, thus creating promotion vacancies. Thanks to greatly improved pay and conditions, and to the deteriorating economic situation outside the police service, very few officers leave before qualifying for a pension, and there is now a tendency for officers to stay in the police, at least until they have completed 30 years' service for maximum pension. An increasing number of officers now choose to serve even longer, until they have reached the ages when police officers must retire (55 years for constables and sergeants, 60 for provincial inspectors and superintendents, 57 for holders of senior ranks in the Metropolitan Police). All this means, of course, that the career opportunities for serving officers are less numerous than they were only a few years ago.

The uniformed policeman
Career prospects

In its turn, this has an effect on the career prospects of all intending police recruits. They should join the service fully understanding that although everyone has an equal opportunity of being selected for the specialist departments, and that the system of promotion by examination and selection is as fair and equitable as it is possible to be, the likelihood is that most officers will remain uniformed constables all their service. It is better that this should be appreciated from the start, because otherwise young officers quickly become disillusioned when they realise what are the odds against promotion, or being selected for specialist duties.

One feature of the uniformed branch which is not, for understandable reasons, highlighted in police recruitment literature, is the fact that the uniform branch tends to be regarded as the least important part of the service by the very people who, frankly, pay lip service to the role of the 'Bobby on the beat'; the senior officers of police forces. Most officers now serving in the uniformed branch will confirm the truth of this statement. It stems, in part, from the misleading glamour which attaches itself to the CID. There is also something intrinsically exciting in the work of the traffic officers, chasing around in their high speed motor cars or on motor cycles. The image of the beat policeman is far more staid and unadventurous.

In the way in which police forces are organised, there is a further cause of the relative inferiority of the uniformed branch in the eyes of authority. Its members sometimes tend to be looked upon more as numbers than as individuals. It is the uniformed constable who has to put up with constant changes of shift and days off, and many other minor inconveniences which are all justified in the name of the 'exigencies of the service', to use a phrase with which the beat constable becomes all too familiar. When next you see television pictures of huge police contingents policing a major demonstration, for example, you may be sure that many of the officers you see have had their normal duties altered, at very short notice, in order to make up the required numbers of police.

The young officer will soon discover that members of the uniform branch, in many cases, are resentful of the attitude which authority displays towards them. Theirs, after all, is the branch of the service which performs the whole range of police duties. The

The uniformed policeman

uniform branch has the highest proportion of shift workers, because the service must provide a twenty-four hour cover for every day of the year. Whilst the specialist departments concern themselves with particular aspects of police work, the uniformed officer is expected to be able to cope, at least in the first instance, with everything. There is a very large area of police activity which is exclusively the responsibility of the uniformed branch, and it is this area which makes the uniformed Bobby such a uniquely important part of the service. The truth of the matter is, that the good beat officer is the most expert specialist of them all; only far too often, the service itself fails to appreciate the fact.

The peace-keeping role

This 'specialist' area of policing can be termed the 'peace-keeping' role of the police, which happens to be the crucial part of the whole police commitment to the public. The beat officer, be he working in a country village or in the heart of the inner city, finds that coping with crime is only an occasional part of his task, even though the great majority of police arrests for crime are made by such officers. For every crime a police officer comes across upon his beat, there are several other incidents every day which require him to be of service to the public. It is unfortunate that, even within the service, these multitudes of demands upon the police are widely regarded as being in some way superfluous and 'not proper police work'. The fact is, they are what policing, or keeping the peace, is all about.

The exciting and glamorous aspects of policing are real enough. A policeman would not be human if he was not elated when he brought off a piece of good police work, and in the police service the art which is prized above all others is that of being a good thief taker. Incidentally, although television and the cinema give a quite different impression, it is the uniform officers rather than the detectives who are the first to be called when a crime is discovered, and as such they are far more likely to be involved in what could be called 'the thrill of the chase' because they are on the scene when a crime is being committed or very shortly afterwards. Most detective work, by definition, begins when the trail is cold. It is only very rarely that detective officers get advance warning of a major crime to enable them to take part in ambushes (and even rarer for these tips from informers to be translated into actual arrests). So being

59

The uniformed policeman

a crime fighter and thief catcher is certainly part and parcel of the job of the uniform patrol officer. But it is only part, and that peace-keeping role is what really counts.

Boredom

One of the biggest drawbacks of routine policing by way of uniform patrols is boredom. Uniformed officers can be assigned to tasks which are monotonous — can you imagine anything more so, for example, than standing for hours on end, day after day, at some special protection point which is part of the security arrangements at Buckingham Palace? Yet this task falls to the policemen on duty there, and when a combination of boredom, complacency and laziness (coupled with some failures of the mechanical alarms) led to an intruder getting into the Queen's bedroom, that one incident did enormous damage to the reputation of the force. If guarding the Sovereign can be boring, however, so can 'plodding' a beat in the hours of darkness, when few people, if any, are about, and the natural tiredness which anyone would feel in the early hours is made worse by the knowledge that there is so much longer to go before the end of the shift. Thanks to the introduction of traffic wardens, policemen nowadays do less than they used to of the grinding work of keeping the streets clear of illegally parked vehicles. But there are many other humdrum but essential tasks which require a police presence and where the chance of excitement is minimal.

Qualities needed to be a good beat patrol constable

So the good beat patrol constable has to find his own ways of keeping his interest alive as much as he can. A lot depends on his own nature. If he is a naturally gregarious person — talking to members of the public, and taking a close interest in the doings of people around him on the beat — getting involved in the life of the community will come naturally to him. But if he is reticent, shy, the kind of person who finds it very difficult to speak to strangers, or unable to concern himself with other people's business, then the likelihood is that he will not make a good beat officer. Inevitably, in the ranks of the uniformed officers at every police station, and

The uniformed policeman

out in the countryside, there are officers who are generally described, rather contemptuously, by their colleagues as 'uniform carriers'. They are people who go through the motions of police work. They do no more than they need to, and as little as they can without attracting criticism or disciplinary action from their superiors. Do not think that all such unsatisfactory police officers are constables, the higher ranks also have their share of such individuals. Whilst the specialist departments, of course, have their share of idlers, moaners, and misfits, their colleagues have at least the satisfaction of being in departments of the force in which they wanted to work and so their own job satisfaction and enthusiasm is not impaired, but young officers spend their early years of service in the uniform branch where the influence of such officers can have a harmful effect. They can dampen enthusiasm and pour scorn on the efforts of supervisors and instructors who are trying to teach recruits the principles of good policing.

There is another side of this particular coin. Because the police service is run on disciplined lines, with a rank structure, it is all too often assumed that an experienced officer who still holds the rank of a constable has somehow 'failed' in his career. This is a foolish generalisation. Yes, there are older officers of the kind mentioned above, but there are also many excellent officers who have remained constables throughout their careers because they themselves have never sought promotion. They have decided that their happiest working level is at that of the constable, and it is from the ranks of such officers that the best community-minded police officers, the ones who are popular and respected by members of the public, are to be found.

The value of experience

The Scarman Inquiry had high praise for such experienced officers. They are the ones who are able to use their own experience of life to bring maturity to their decisions. Family men who have themselves experienced some of the pressures of married life are better fitted to handle some of the many domestic disputes with which every beat officer has to deal. When an officer has himself known the problems of starting married life in financial hardship, inadequate housing, trouble with 'in-laws', it helps when what is really needed at such times is advice and finding ways to get couples reconciled.

The uniformed policeman
Young police officers are at a disadvantage when called, say, to a fight between a married couple because they have no personal experience to draw upon, and experience is the best of all police tutors. Again, the police officer with children of his own, or who has had to cope with the family strains imposed when generations clash, as between teenagers and their parents, is more likely to understand and know how to deal with the problem of establishing his authority as a police officer when dealing with youngsters on the streets. The art is in securing respect without being autocratic and officious.

Many of the tasks which fall to the beat officer appear to be light years removed from the public's broad perception of a policeman's job. We have all read of the officers who have to act as emergency midwives when babies arrive unexpectedly, or respond to equally urgent sudden demands for assistance. But what of the other, sadder side of life? Every year, thousands of people, fathers, husbands, mothers, wives and children, are killed on the roads. Invariably, it is a police officer who has to knock on some household's door and break the news of stark tragedy to people he has never seen before and may never see again. A policeman knows that these are the moments when, no matter how many times he has done such a task before, the stress it puts upon him, as well as upon the bereaved relatives, is enormous. Any police officer would say that this is one of the tasks which he dreads, just as he knows that all too often it is only the policeman who can do anything about it.

One of the realities of modern living is that, in spite of the development of social services under the welfare state, real proverty is not far below the surface. Policemen see examples of deprivation all the time when they work in inner city areas; one-parent families where young mothers struggle to bring up children on wholly inadequate incomes; elderly people who are either too proud or unable to ask for the additional social benefits to which they are entitled; cases of child neglect and cruelty, and so forth. The police are not there to deal with the remedies, if any, for such problems, but very often it is due to the fact that a case comes to the notice of a police officer, and he in turn is able to alert the social workers, that help comes at last to the people concerned. Sometimes that help never arrives. Police officers know all about having to break down the door of a flat or house where some old person who lived alone has not been seen for some time, and eventually either the

The uniformed policeman

neighbours or tradesmen have suggested that 'something might have happened'. Invariably, what has happened is that the old person has died, neglected by the community.

It is possible nowadays to be rather more positive in discussing the work of the uniformed branch of the service, because the recent concentration of public interest in all things to do with the police service, has produced a broad concensus in which the public appears to be saying that the most appreciated aspect of the police service is the very one which, in the past, the police service itself has valued the least.

The beat officer

Thanks to the rapid expansion in the size of the police service, the 'Bobby on the beat' has come back into fashion. It seems hard to believe now that, during the lean years of the sixties and seventies, the prevailing wisdom in the higher ranks of the police service was that the constable on the beat had had his day. He had no role to play in an increasingly mobile and technological society. The reasoning behind this philosophy made some sense at the time: crime was rising rapidly and police forces saw no prospect of ever getting sufficient manpower to maintain the system of beat policing which had been the natural order of policing up to 1939. Crime prevention and detection were considered to be the most important of the primary objectives of the police service, and therefore the answer seemed to lie in greater mobility for the police officer, which meant putting individual officers in motor cars, coupled with better technology, of which the most important development was the personal radio in the sixties. Prior to this, beat officers had only the telephone as a means of keeping in touch with the police station from which they operated. The personal radio meant that beat officers were put in permanent contact with their police base, and in turn this has led to beat officers undertaking far more duties during each shift than would their counterparts of earlier days. Some police officers, old enough to recall the days before personal radios, panda cars, and computers, believe that technology has not been an unmixed blessing. It follows, for example, that if the work load each day of the beat officer has increased, then he is spending more and more of his time in responding to calls for action, and less in the basic duty of preventive patrolling. Although this

The uniformed policeman

preventive role is unglamorous and seemingly unproductive, it is the very presence and sight of a patrolling police officer which provides that reassurance for members of the public who feel most at risk.

During the lean years, the beat system was maintained only by coupling up single beats, giving individual police officers far more 'ground' to cover and making them less effective in that social role of crime preventers. The problem was felt just as keenly in the villages, where police forces were forced to accept that maintaining a permanent 'village Bobby' in each village was not cost effective. In any case, the villages themselves were suffering from big population losses. Much as the remaining inhabitants regretted the loss of 'their' police officers, the economic facts of life made unavoidable a policy of grouping villages together and making one officer cover areas that were once patrolled by several village constables.

Paradoxically, the acknowledged value and popularity of the village constable forms the basis of a widespread form of modern urban policing. In the past, towns have been policed on a beat system in which they were divided up into beats which were patrolled by different officers. Now the concept of officers living and working on a beat which has been permanently allocated to them has been adopted in many forces, including the Metropolitan police. Of course, the ideal would be to have every 'Home Beat' or 'Neighbourhood' constable living on his beat, but this is unlikely to happen for a wide variety of reasons. The days when police officers had to live in police houses and could be moved from home to home by the force, are long gone. The great majority of police officers are now home owners, with only a small percentage living in the remaining 'police houses', these mostly being village officers living in police houses with offices attached to them. Because police officers can exercise a broad choice (they are paid a generous rent allowance to assist them with house purchase) they naturally will not choose to live with their families in some areas where social problems are great. This situation is not going to change, if only because police officers see no reason why their families should be housed to suit the needs of the police service. Even in less difficult neighbourhoods, police officers prefer to separate their private and professional lives by not living 'on the job'. They do not want their families to be involved in their role as police officers.

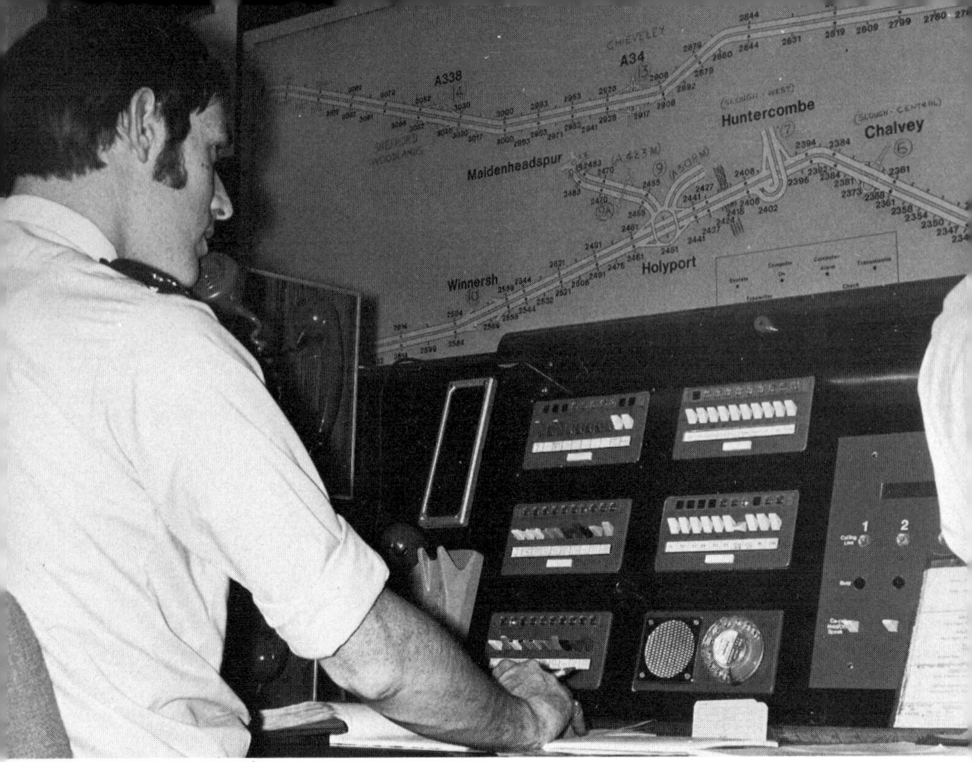

CHIEVELEY
A338
A34
Huntercombe
Chalvey
Maidenheadspur
Winnersh
Holyport

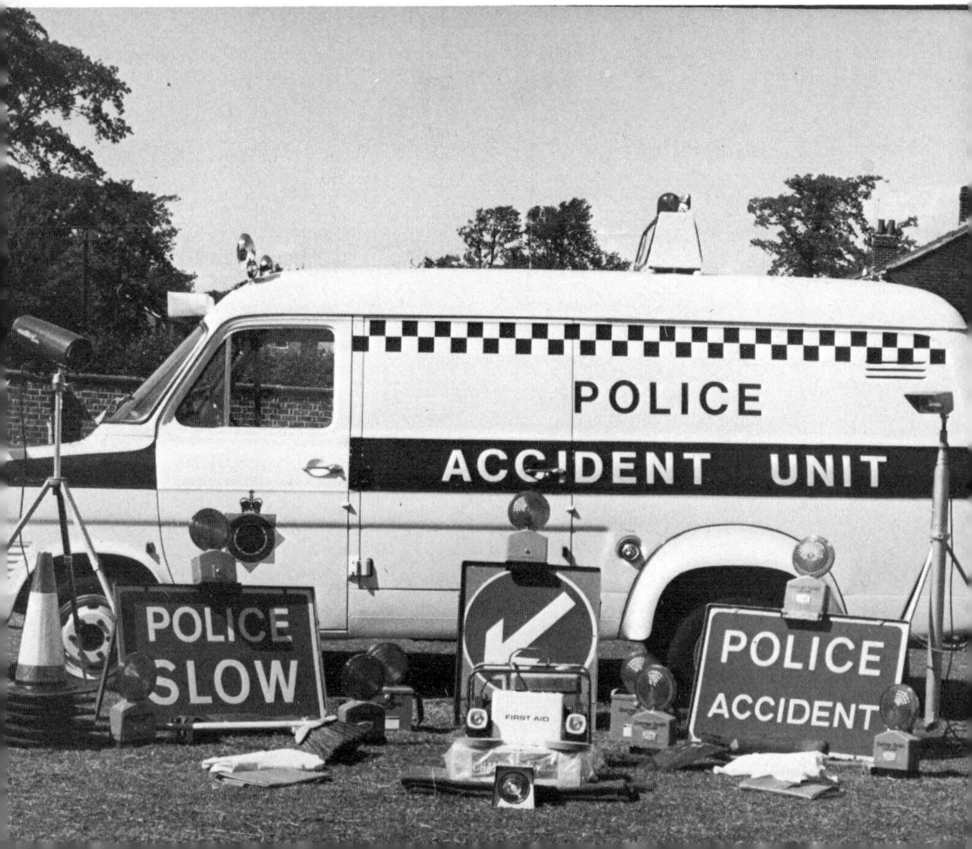

POLICE
ACCIDENT UNIT
POLICE
SLOW
POLICE
ACCIDENT
FIRST AID

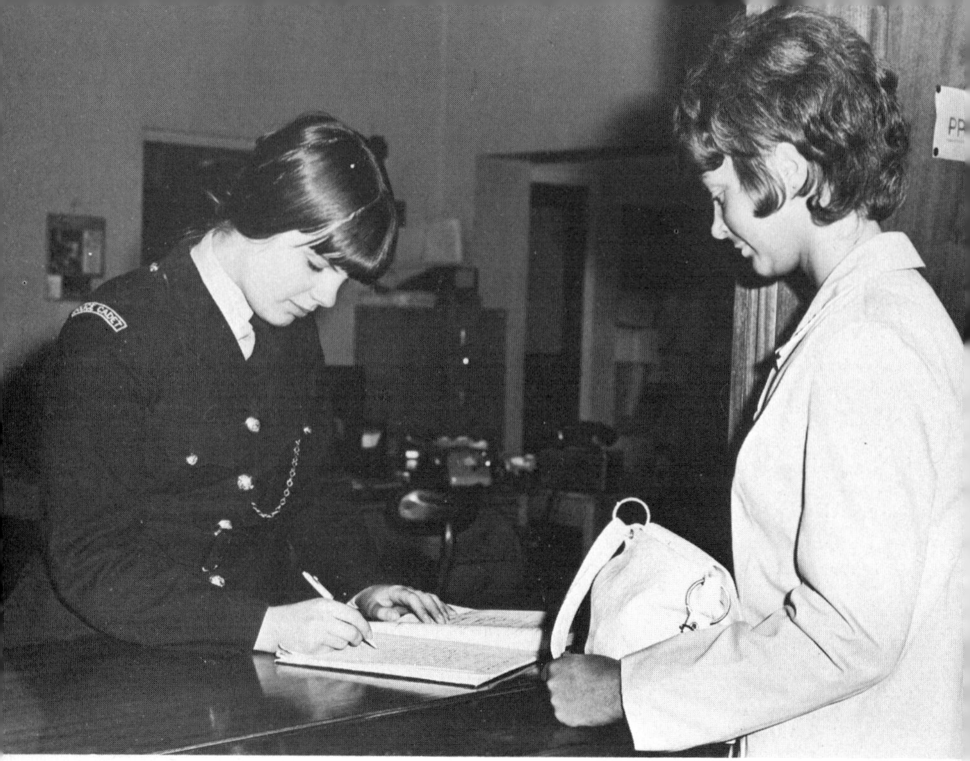

The uniformed policeman

Nevertheless, the officer who is assigned to a permanent beat is expected to get to know the community he serves as thoroughly as he can. The idea is that the local people should come to regard that constable as 'their' policeman. Obviously, not all police officers are temperamentally suited to this kind of police work and some care has to be taken by senior officers when selecting officers to become 'Home Beat' or 'Neighbourhood' officers. The ideal person for this kind of policing has to be dedicated and possess some qualities of leadership. He should be able to work with all the other people who perform a service for the community; the social workers, the school staffs; the local doctor; shopkeepers, publicans; local councillors, and so on. Above all, he must get to know as many individual members of the public as he can and remember at all times that he is bound to become the person by whom those members of the public judge the police force as a whole.

Community policing

Community policing is a term which has come to be applied to systems of policing which have been adopted by all police forces in Britain, and which are aimed at bringing the police and the public closer together, with the common objective of reducing crime in the community and increasing public confidence in the rule of law. It is difficult to say where and when community policing actually began in Britain. Several forces and chief officers have laid claim to having pioneered the concept. Others say that the idea came from pioneering work done in the United States of America. Who began it is less important than saying what community policing is, and unquestionably, the chief officer whose name became synonymous with community policing was Mr John Alderson, who for about ten years until 1982, was the Chief Constable of Devon and Cornwall. Mr Alderson was an articulate chief constable who wrote and lectured extensively upon the subject and, in the process, became a controversial public figure because he spoke out against what he saw as demands for more autocratic and repressive forms of policing and social control. In 1982 he appeared to part company altogether from the majority of his brother chief constables, when he accused some of them of wishing to 'tool up to make war on the public'. He was referring to the police reaction to the 1981 riots and in particular to demands for such things as plastic bullets, water

The uniformed policeman

cannons and other methods of enabling the police to attack rather than contain, and deal with rioters by less aggressive means. The critics of Mr Alderson were particularly resentful of his intervention, including the 'tooling up' allegation, in the Scarman inquiry into the causes of the Brixton riots and the policing of the area. One chief officer protested at the time: 'We have been practising community policing for years. Unlike John Alderson we do not go around shouting about it from the rooftops!' When Mr Alderson retired shortly afterwards, it was unfortunately the case that his alienation from the mainstream of police opinion tended to overshadow his considerable efforts to promote community policing, to the extent where his advocacy of the system was, in itself, one of the handicaps it had to overcome when seeking to find general acceptance in the police service. Having said this, I freely acknowledge my indebtedness to Mr Alderson in the following passages dealing with the subject of community policing.

The system has been developed in a number of different but broadly similar ways. Variations between one form of community policing and another are usually due to variations between communities and neighbourhoods. What works very well in a rural and largely middle-class village, for example, is not what is required in a deprived multi-racial area of the inner city. Yet community policing has a record of success almost everywhere it has been tried out, in areas which are as different from each other as middle-class enclaves in villages and cities, to some of the most difficult areas of the inner cities. For example, the Handsworth district of Birmingham, a heavily multi-racial area, once had the reputation of being the place in Britain where really serious clashes between the police and the coloured population were most likely to occur. Although Handsworth never erupted on the scale afterwards seen in Brixton and Toxteth, there were violent episodes there long before things got out of hand in the other places. Community policing was considered to be the answer, and although the initial reaction of the community was suspicious and hostile, the police, by dint of good leadership and the exercise of a great deal of patience, built up an atmosphere of much greater trust, largely based upon having permanent beat officers and encouraging ordinary members of the public to make greater use of the police as people who were interested in helping the public. It was considered to be a sign of the success of these efforts that, when the rest of

The uniformed policeman

the inner cities experienced street disturbances in 1981, the people of Handsworth remained calm.

As developed along the Devon and Cornwall pattern, community policing begins with the identification of a particular area. It could, in a county force, be a village. In a town, it could be a neighbourhood with a name, such as 'the High Street area', or a large housing estate. John Alderson, whilst acknowledging that the problems of inner city areas were greater than those of middle-class urban districts and far removed from the villages, insisted that it was possible for community policing to operate anywhere. He was fond of talking about 'the village in the city' and, as city dwellers will know, it is quite true that people tend to think first of their own locality, the people they know, the schools, churches, pubs and shops in their immediate vicinity. To be effective, community policing needs to be kept at levels which small groups, and one police officer, can operate.

One way of starting the schemes has been to invite members of the local community to a meeting where the police tell them about the problems which the police face in their neighbourhoods; the level of crime, particularly burglaries and vandalism. It is then explained that the force proposes to appoint a particular constable as 'their' police officer, and ways are then discussed of how all the social agencies and people providing a service in the community, can work with the police to prevent crime and make people living in the neighbourhood feel safer. Thus, the community constable is expected to spend most of his working time, and a great deal of his own time in many cases, in working with youth groups, sports clubs, old people's organisations, and so on, with special emphasis on the schools.

Community policing relies on the willingness of members of the local community to work with the police. It requires, also, that people should feel that they belong to the neighbourhood, wish to remain living in the neighbourhood, and have a stake in it. Not all these conditions are satisfied in all cases. Many people living in the crime and problem-ridden inner city, for example, feel none of these things towards their homes. Their ambition is to live somewhere else. But, in the main, the latent community spirit of ordinary people can be tapped by enthusiastic police officers.

Critics of the philosophy of community policing are concerned about the change of what they regard as the primary object of the

The uniformed policeman

police force. They say that it is a policeman's job to fight crime, catch criminals, protect life and property, but not to act as a social worker and to concern himself with problems which he and the police service cannot solve. It is also said that the 'soft' image of the community constable contrasts sharply with other developments in modern policing, in which the police have had to form special squads and use riot gear to quell disorder. On the political left, people who are naturally sceptical about the police are extremely suspicious of community policing. They see it as a means by which the police will gain the confidence of the community by building up a network of informers and spies. If this sounds far fetched, it is true that a very well known politician, Mr Ted Knight, the leader of Lambeth Council in London at the time of the Brixton riots, says that 'community policing means having a copper's nark on every street corner'.

Whatever forms of policing are used now and in the immediate future, the police are bound to concentrate on the best available means of maintaining that close contact between the police and the public without which they cannot hope to 'police by consent'. So, community policing, home beats, neighbourhood watch, call it what one will, is likely to be the pattern of regular policing to which most police recruits will be introduced.

Women police

About one in every ten police officers is a woman. Women in the police service have found their careers greatly affected by the Equal Pay Act and the Sex Discrimination Act, because until these came along during the nineteen seventies, women were very much 'second class citizens' as far as the police service was concerned.

It was not until the First World War, almost 100 years after the formation of the police service, that women were first permitted to wear police uniforms. At first they were called Women Patrols or Auxiliaries. For a time there were two separate and bitterly antipathetic groups operating in London, vying with each other for the official recognition of the force. It was the War which brought about the need for some kind of force which would look after the moral welfare of young women working in the munitions factories and deal with the widespread increase in prostitution in the vicinity of the huge Army camps. The women's suffrage movement, which enthusiastically supported the war effort in the expectation of having their campaign for women to have the vote rewarded, took a great interest in the new women police and several of the first officers of the corps were prominent suffragettes.

The deeply conservative police force of the time, and especially the Chief Constables, gave only grudging support to the women police and very few policemen would admit that there was a permanent role for women officers to play. It was claimed by male officers that police work was something that could only be done by men. A policeman, it was pointed out, had to be out in all weathers, and women were far too delicate to withstand the rigours of the British climate out of doors all day and night; policemen had to rely on physical strength and a woman would be no match for a drunken ruffian in a street fight; the police often came into contact with the seamiest and most sordid aspects of life, and women of good character should be shielded from such things (for example, even experienced senior police officers were shocked by suggestions that a useful role for a woman police officer would be in the investigation of sexual offences and illegal abortions. Such officers argued that respectable ladies should be protected from having to confront the depravity and beastliness of men).

Women police

After the War ended, most of the forces which had formed Women's Patrols disbanded them on the grounds that they were no longer needed. Things appeared to be better in London, where the then Commissioner, General Sir Nevil Macready, recognised one of the two competing groups and allowed these to become the nucleus of the force's first policewomen's corps. The dozen ladies chosen for this pioneer work all came from 'good families' and were far better educated than most of the men with whom they would have to work. It was typical of the official attitude towards them that they obtained their first uniforms, modelled as far as posible on those of the men, but with ankle length skirts and lace-up boots, from the exclusive Knightsbridge store, Harrods. Still, it was a beginning and the Metropolitan women police enjoyed the powerful support of Lady Astor, the first woman to be elected and take her seat in the House of Commons. It was Lady Astor who fought hard to persuade the Government not to disband the policewomen in London when Macready's successor, General Horwood, wished to do so as an economy measure. The Metropolitan senior officers appeared to share the views of provincial chief constables, that women had no real place in the service. Lady Astor was only partly successful in her campaign to keep the policewomen. The Home Secretary agreed to keep a much reduced, almost token force of women officers.

Soon after this blow fell, however, a public scandal broke over the force when outraged Members of Parliament protested about an incident in which a young woman, who was involved in a court case involving a prominent person, was questioned by senior detectives at Scotland Yard. The incident led to a Royal Commission being set up to inquire into police powers, and it became obvious that the incident would have been less serious had not a policewoman, who was accompanying the young woman to the police interview, been ordered to leave the room in which it took place. From the time of the Royal Commission onwards, there was less talk of getting rid of policewomen altogether. Even so, it was not until the end of the Second World War that all forces began to employ women police officers, and then there was no question of abandoning discrimination altogether. For example, until the late nineteen seventies the proportion of women to men in the service was only about one in twenty. Until the Equal Pay Act, women were paid only ninety per cent of the men's rates.

The Sex Discrimination Act

The most important distinction, which was ended by the Sex Discrimination Act, was in the way in which women were employed in the police. They were organised as a separate department of each force, although a very few women worked as detective officers in the criminal investigation departments, and an even smaller number could be found dotted around the traffic departments, working as dog handlers or as mounted officers. The policewomen's departments had their own rank structure and did not compete for promotion with their male colleagues. At this time, women did not perform the full range of police duties in many forces, but were regarded as specialists in matters to do with women and children.

The Sex Discrimination Act meant that the police service could no longer make official distinctions between male and female officers. An immediate consequence was that the policewomen's departments had to be disbanded and women officers were entitled to be employed on the full range of police duties. The separate rank structure for women had to go as well, and from then on women have had to take their chance on promotion with men.

These changes were not altogether popular with the police, either men or women, at the time they were introduced. The chief officers and the Police Federation, which represents the ranks below Superintendent, had urged that the police service should be exempted from the requirements of the Sex Discrimination Act, and they used arguments which were reminiscent of the attitudes of the chief officers of 50 years before. Much emphasis was placed on the lack of physical strength of women officers, and it was said that whereas the men in the service were pursuing a lifetime career, most of the women officers were not career officers, because the great majority of policewomen left the service after a few years in order to get married. Parliament and the supporters of the Act were not impressed by these arguments, and the police were refused exemption from the terms of the Act.

Yet neither were the women officers, who were serving at the time of the Act, entirely happy with the compulsory 'integration' made necessary by the new law. The previous arrangements favoured the small minority of dedicated career officers amongst the women. They had their own rank structure and they could see their future

Women police

prospects fairly clearly. Now they would have to compete with men for advancement, and risk the hidden prejudice and discrimination which no Act of Parliament can eliminate entirely. As some of the women career officers complained at the time, they would now find that it was not enough to deserve promotion on their own merits as women police officers; they would have to overcome the handicap of being women when competing, on supposedly equal terms, with male colleagues. Although by no means all the women officers shared these fears, to some extent they appear to have been borne out by events. It was not until 1983, for example, that a woman officer secured appointment to a Chief Officer's rank in competition with men, when a woman was appointed to an assistant chief constable's post in the Merseyside Police. In contrast, the women in the Metropolitan Police were under the command of a woman Commander (equivalent of an assistant chief constable in the provinces) before the Act, but when the holder of this rank retired, the highest post held by a woman in the Metropolitan Police was, at that time, chief superintendent. It may well be inevitable that one day a woman will be a chief constable, or even that some future Commissioner of Police of the Metropolis will be a woman, but current attitudes suggest that women will take longer to reach the very top in the police service than in most other occupations. To a large degree, this must be attributed to the prevailingly masculine overtones of the service itself, something which was heavily criticised in 1983 by the Policy Studies Institute's report on the Metropolitan Police, and this aspect of police life will be commented on later in this chapter.

Dealing with women and children

A more valid argument about women in the police service, which was put forward at the time of the Sex Discrimination Act, was that the existing policewomen's departments played an indispensible role in dealing with women's and children's matters, and that over the years they had acquired experience and expertise that could not be replaced. This question came into greater prominence within a very short time after the Act was passed. The police found themselves being fiercely criticised for their actions and attitudes with regard to domestic violence against women, the battered wives question, and in relation to the investigation of alleged cases of

Women police

rape. The issue was highlighed by a national television programme which showed male detective officers questioning a woman who had complained of rape, and showing her scant sympathy. Ironically, the women who led the outcry against the police on this occasion, may have been the staunchest supporters of the Act which had led police forces to dismantle the policewomen's departments. Policewomen were no longer receiving the specialised training in matters pertaining to women and children and, by being employed on the general range of police duties, the experience built up over the years was lost to the service. In the wake of the criticism, and in response to the growing insistence of women's organisations that the police should do more to protect women from the risk of male violence, some chief officers began a few years ago to revive the old departments to deal with women's and children's questions, but to staff them with men and women officers. It was noticeable that, whereas when the Sex Discrimination Act came into force the majority of serving women officers were unhappy with the changes, by the early nineteen eighties majority opinion amongst the women officers was that they would resist any return to the old system, under which they were virtually excluded from the full range of police duties.

Dealing with violence

It would be wrong to assume, however, that the police service is now wholly reconciled to the idea that women officers are in all respects the equals of their male colleagues. Most chief constables, for example, will not deploy women officers in situations such as violent political or industrial demonstrations, or sudden outbreaks of rioting. The police support units, set up to deal with outbreaks of disorder, do not contain women officers. The argument in support of this policy is that a male police officer, when having to cope with violence, has quite enough on his hands without having to keep one eye upon his weaker female colleague alongside him. A minority of forces do employ women in potentially violent situations, such as policing football grojnds, but generally the use of women officers at demonstrations and similar events is confined to a second line role; dealing with women prisoners and casualties, record processing, communication and liaison, and similar tasks. Those chief constables who refuse to discriminate between men and

Women police

women when it comes to deploying police in 'confrontation' situations, justify their policy by saying that in this age of equal pay and opportunities between the sexes, women must either do the full range of police duties or leave the service, even if as in some cases, this means requiring a woman officer to perform street duty on her own at night. In any case, it must be stressed that women are not by any means immune from the dangers of police duties. They are quite often used as 'decoys' when the police are attempting to trap a rapist who has carried out a series of attacks on women, and no police officer, male or female, can ever be sure that even the most routine incident will not be transferred in an instant into a violent and potentially very dangerous situation. There seemed to be no danger, for example, when a young woman detective officer, Maureen Martin, went to arrest a petty offender at his home in Northumberland in 1982, but he suddenly produced a shotgun and wounded her so badly that she is now a paraplegic. On the other hand, Constable Jane Arbuthnot of the Metropolitan Police became the first policewoman to be murdered in this country (excluding Northern Ireland) when she went with her men and women colleagues to investigate a bomb warning in Knightsbridge at Christmas 1983 and was killed when a car exploded. Cases are quite common of policewomen being decorated or commended by chief officers for individual acts of bravery, either in dealing with armed or disturbed and violent criminals, or in performing rescues at great personal risk.

Whatever the merits of the constant argument about the role of women in dealing with violence, it is now becoming recognised that there are many situations in which a woman officer, acting on her own, is capable of defusing a potentially violent incident because, as a woman, her approach to the problem, and to individuals concerned in it, is likely to be less aggressive and more sympathetic than would be the case if a male police officer was asked to deal with it. This has been borne out by several important pieces of research into the police, including the 1983 Policy Studies Institute report mentioned previously.

Qualities needed to become a policewoman

A young woman who is contemplating a police career would be well advised to find out as much about the nature of police work as she can, before making a decision to pursue a serious application. This applies to any police applicant, of course, but in the case of a woman applicant this advice is more than the usual conventional suggestion. *Policing is different!* It makes no concessions to femininity. For example, almost every other job in the public service, and many in the private sector, encourage women to go on working after marriage. Not so the police service. Until quite recently, police forces actually made women resign on marriage, a practice that is now illegal, but the service has set its collective (masculine) face against making special arrangements for women members. When, some years ago, a Parliamentary Committee was so concerned at the fact that the overwhelming majority of women officers resigned after only about three years' service, and suggested that this wastage of training and experience could be reduced if women who had left on marriage, or in order to have children, were to be offered the opportunity to return to the service as part time employees, the opposition from the service was total, and none were more vehement in their objections than the small minority of career women officers. Even today, at a time when 'job sharing' is a concept which is strongly supported by the women's movement, there has been no such move in the police service and nor is there likely to be one.

The 1983 case of alleged sex discrimination in the Metropolitan Police, in which a woman constable won a case in which she claimed that her senior officers had discriminated against her on sexual grounds, should not be regarded as an isolated example. This officer was employed in the traffic department, and she was transferred against her wish to the uniform patrol branch after her senior officer told her that she got on too well with her male working partner. It was not alleged that she was having an affair with the other officer, a married man, but the senior officer who informed her of her transfer said that he was taking this action to avoid any such thing happening! It was significant that, of the two 'blameless' officers involved in this decision, it was the woman officer whom it was decided to remove from traffic duties, not the man. This case came to light because of the unusual strength of character displayed by the woman officer and her male colleague, who were prepared to challenge the decision of their superior officers at an outside tribunal — something that is frowned upon inside the service, and which lead to subsequent difficulties for the

Women police

male officer who supported the woman officer's case before the tribunal. Many other cases in which women officers feel themselves to be the victims of sexual discrimination do not come to light because the officers concerned do not go to the same lengths to secure redress.

The Policy Studies Institute Report

The Policy Studies Institute Report on the Metropolitan Police provided some revealing glimpses of what life can be like for some women officers. The Report spoke of a pervading cult of masculinity in the force:

> 'Policewomen now pursue careers formally on an equal footing with policemen, but find it difficult to fit in with an organisation that still has much of the culture of a male preserve .... Bawdy talk is a kind of game among groups of men in which they play, in their imagination, the role of a man triumphing over a woman. For example, an older PC said that "in the old days" WPCs when they first arrived at a police station were always stamped "on the bare bum" with the station rubber stamp. This fantasy neatly symbolises the three chief impulses that animate this kind of conversational game; the treatment of a woman as a thing; the humiliation of a woman and the sexual assault upon her. Talk about women on this level is pervasive among groups of men in the Met; much of it is far more lurid and extreme than the small example quoted. It often continues when women are present, though the men may then switch to competing for the attention of the woman (if she is considered attractive).'

Of course, women encounter precisely the same attitudes in most other occupations in which the proportion of males far outnumbers females. The PSI comments about aggressive and offensive male chauvinism in the force were considered shocking and sensational when the Report appeared, but on this, as with many other aspects of the police service, it must never be assumed that policemen, as soon as they become such, are transformed into men who are free of all masculine vices or prejudices.

In other words, a young woman wishing to join the police service

Women police

must understand that male chauvinism and its unpleasant manifestations are things which she must expect to face, and she must decide for herself if she is the kind of person who can overcome it. All that can be said here is that, notwithstanding the comments in the PSI report, a surprising number of women seem to find job satisfaction and personal fulfilment in the police service, and they do not have to sacrifice their femininity in order to achieve these aims.

At the funeral of Yvonne Fletcher, the young constable who was murdered by a gunman at the Lybian Embassy in London in 1984, the Bishop of Salisbury had this to say:

> 'Our human defenders against such evil are our police forces, and this duty puts them in frequent danger. But death may strike, as it did in St James's Square, when no one could have expected it. To understand that, but to go about your job just the same calls for a special light-hearted, long distance kind of courage.
>
> It is because the police, by the very nature of their calling, are to be on the side of right against wrong, and because over the years they have built up these high traditions of courage and service, that fine young people like Yvonne Fletcher have but one ambition, to wear the uniform with pride.'

Leadership

One of the things which the police service has in common with the armed forces is the need to have first class leadership. This is not the kind of leadership which calls to mind the cavalry officer flourishing his sabre at the enemy lines and shouting 'Charge!' as he leads a headlong gallop through the bursting shells. It is firm, cool, leadership by example. What leaders at any level in the police service need is the ability to gain the respect of those for whom they are responsible, and the first and foremost quality which helps to acquire this respect is all round professional competence.

Police officers know whether or not the person giving the orders is capable of carrying them out himself. There are officers holding rank in the police service who may well have all the professional knowledge that is required, but who are not greatly respected (to put it politely) by those under their command, because it is known that they lack judgement, or are prone to panic in emergencies, are indecisive, or even because their personal courage is doubted. In every walk of life, some people are promoted above the level of their abilities. The police service cannot be expected to devise a system of promotion which is capable of guaranteeing that candidates who, at the time that they are selected for promotion appear fully qualified and personally capable of assuming the responsibilities, will in practice fail to measure up to the required standards. So the police service, as with any other job, has its bad and mediocre managers and leaders, just as it has some very good ones.

The Police Constable

Because the police service has to have ranks above constable to make a disciplined service function effectively, the public has a tendency to look upon constables sometimes as police officers who have 'failed' to gain promotion. This is very far from the truth, and there are many first class constables who make a positive contribution to the success of the service who have never sought promotion. Some of these officers would find themselves much less

Leadership

effective if they had to worry about the additional responsibilities which go with rank, but their value has been best expressed in recent years by the introduction of the 'tutor constable' project, by which older officers offer guidance and the benefit of their experience to recruits from the training schools. This is leadership by example, demonstrating that one does not need to be promoted to offer leadership qualities.

The ranking system

Another common misconception about police ranks is that they are equated with the armed forces. The police service may in the time of Robert Peel have adopted the title 'Sergeant', which is the one police rank to bear the same nomenclature as an Army rank, but in keeping with the determination of Peel to have a 'civilian' service, the other ranks were called 'Inspector' and 'Superintendent'. The armed forces differentiate between 'officers', who hold the Queen's Commission, and 'other ranks', but no such distinction is appropriate for the police. This said, the service has itself brought about a social distinction, which many consider unfortunate, between officers of the rank of inspector and above, and constables and sergeants. For example; constables and sergeants are required to address inspectors and higher ranks as 'Sir' (or Ma'am) and to salute them. Some forces have carried the distinction further by having 'senior officers'' dining rooms which exclude 'the lower ranks'. The Police Federation, the organisation which represents all ranks below superintendent, has opposed this 'officer class' mentality, arguing that anything which is done to enhance the status of the higher ranks in the police service inevitably diminishes the status, and therefore the professional pride, of the constables. Of course, the only genuine way in which the police service can increase the public estimation of the quality of senior officers is by ensuring that their performance as professional police officers and as leaders is first class. This is the primary purpose of the Police College and the systems of staff appraisal and selection for promotion.

Duties and responsibilities

What are the duties and responsibilities of the ranks of sergeant

Leadership

and above in the police? Here, let several officers speak for themselves. The reader will see, from what they say about their jobs, that each rank in the police service carries specific levels of responsibility, each requiring a higher level of management skills than the rank below it.

Recruit A 'A' joined the West Midlands Police on leaving a grammar school at 19. He has six O levels and his original idea of going to university to read Law fell through when his A level results were not good enough. A close friend in the force urged him to apply, and he was accepted. Now some six months after first putting on the uniform, he gives this assessment of his choice.

'I still don't know whether this is the job that I want to do for the rest of my life. Most of the people I was with at the training centre were what you could call "committed". There were a few ex-police cadets who knew all about the job. Some of them were sons and daughters of police officers, and we had some from the Army, older people, who intended to settle down in a new career. Then there were those, like me, who decided rather late that we would like to be policemen.

'When I went for my interview they asked me a lot of searching questions about commitment, and because I'd been warned that they would, I suppose I gave them the kind of answers they wanted to hear. You see, I wanted at that time to have a job, not be on the dole like so many of my friends at school, even ones with good results. I know one or two people with degrees who can't get work. The police offer good pay and security. They don't make you redundant. But it wasn't just that. I've always been interested in crime, and I didn't want a nine to five job Monday to Friday, doing the same old thing.

'I don't want to put anyone off, but I didn't like the training centre. I thought there were too many petty rules and regulations; too much marching about, saluting and standing to attention to senior officers.

'Some people packed it in after a few weeks at the centre. They wouldn't put up with it. I seriously considered doing the same once or twice. Then, half way through the course, things began to change as far as I was concerned. I don't exactly know why, but I think it was the "police atmosphere" getting to me. By this time,

Leadership

we were talking and thinking like policemen. I found myself talking about a chap I knew to other policemen, and I said, "this civvie". What I mean is, there's no getting away from the fact that there is such a thing as the police world and the police family. I found myself looking forward to getting through the course and actually going out on the beat as a constable.

'I've been at this station for three months. It's one of the busiest in the force and there are dozens of things going on all the time. Of course, I still haven't done much on my own. They put you with an older man who shows you round his beat, and we are supervised pretty closely. But if the sergeants and inspectors think you are doing your best, then they are very helpful. I've been in a couple of hairy incidents. I was going home one night, not in uniform, when a crowd of yobboes came dashing out of a pub, chasing this chap. He had a knife in his hand, and there was an almighty punch up. I went in without thinking and ended up holding on to one of them on the ground, but his mates started putting the boot in. Luckily, the landlord had phoned the police and two cars came up in no time. We got the chap I was holding in a van. I thought I'd done well, but next day the inspector said I should have gone for help first. He pointed out that it was just good luck that other police were on their way, I could have been kicked unconscious and they would have had no one for it. As it was, there were two arrests for grievous bodily harm and one charge might still turn out to be attempted murder.

'The other was when I was on night duty and I was in a beat car with another constable. This car came round a corner nearly on two wheels. We saw two young kids in it and my mate said, "Come on, it's a knocked off car." I used my personal radio to let the local station know what was happening, and we followed it. You are not supposed to chase anything in the beat cars. It's skilled work driving fast, and if you have a crash you are in trouble. But this lad was a good driver and they weren't. We headed them off easily and they mounted the pavement. They were high on some drugs or other, and one of them was a big lad who wanted to fight. He went berserk and it took us both to get the cuffs on him.

'It is times like that which, although you know there's a risk, you enjoy it. I suppose we are not expected to be pleased when we lock someone up, but we are. It's because that is what your job is, fighting crime. Yes, you do like to think you have got a "good

Leadership

prisoner". That means he's not just a simple drunk or a sneak thief, but someone who's done something serious, or someone whom the force has been after for a good while. When a couple of the lads on my turn caught a local burglar, the atmosphere in the station was great, because we had all wanted to catch him. He had been at it for months but had just got away half a dozen times. Then he walked round a corner, slap into them, and he had the property on him.

'So far, I think being out on the beat is great, but I haven't made up my mind yet as to whether I still want to be a policeman in 30 years time. I've noticed a change in my friends off the job. They don't trust me. It's nothing outright anti-police, but I get the feeling that they are watching what they say. It's ridiculous. they aren't the criminal type, yet they are wary of me. I sometimes wonder when I hear people going on about the police, how much they support them. In this job, you soon learn that people might respect you, but they don't want to be close friends. I suppose it's only to be expected, because we have to uphold the law, but you do begin to feel a bit of the odd one out. If I can accept that, and learn to live with it, then I'll stay as long as I enjoy the job. On the other hand, they may decide that they don't want to keep me. Until I get my two years' probation in, they can get rid of me at any time.'

Sergeant B serves in a busy urban force. He left school at sixteen and was a miner for four years. Ten years ago, because the local pit was closed down and he saw no future for himself in the coal industry, he applied to join his local police force. He was accepted and for the first seven years he worked as a beat constable and, for a few months before he was promoted to sergeant, he was a police driver.

'Studying never came easily to me, so I had to work hard to pass the promotion examinations. Whilst I was studying, my wife had to keep the children quiet and sometimes I wondered if being promoted was worth all the domestic trouble that I had at that time. I was pleased when I passed and even more pleased, of course, when I was promoted. I had to appear before a promotion board. The funny thing was, I did not think I had done well enough when I went in for that interview and I expected to be told that I had failed that time.

Leadership

'Being promoted meant a move away from the shift I had worked with in traffic. This force has a policy of moving people on promotion. It is very rare that a man stays in the same place, or with the same people. I suppose this helps you to start acting as a sergeant instead of a constable. I mean, it's not easy to be having a drink with your mates on the shift one day, and then have to tell one of them off the next day because you've found him doing something he shouldn't have done.

'I was lucky in one sense, because I was transferred to a station fairly near to my home. I'm an owner occupier and the children have settled in at their school. Some people have to move to the other end of the force area when they are promoted, which could mean uprooting your family, trying to sell one house and buy another, and if your wife is working, she has to try and find a job in another area, which is easier said than done. I would say that a lot of policemen turn down promotion because they just can't put up with the hassle it causes in the family. Of course, the money is better, but the difference between the top pay of a constable and what a sergeant gets isn't all that much. At the beginning, when you first get promoted, you are hardly any better off, so I do not think that many people want promotion to get more money, not at the sergeant level, anyway.

'When I was a young constable, I had a lot of help from one sergeant who was in charge of my shift. You could always go to him for advice about a case you had, whether it was reporting someone for driving without due care and attention, or what the correct charge was for someone you'd arrested. One or two of the sergeants I had just did not want to know. They were no help to constables and all they wanted was to get their time in with the least bother to themselves. We soon got to know who were the good sergeants and which ones were useless.

'I try to take an interest in all the constables on my shift. We have a dozen altogether, including three girls, but after you've taken account of days off, annual leave, courses, and the odd one who is off sick, you're down to half a dozen at the most and sometimes less than that.

'A few months back, on nights, we surrounded a warehouse because one of the beat men had spotted a car belonging to a local villain parked near the back of the place. When we went in with the key holder, there were five of them there, just getting a load of stuff

Leadership

ready for a lorry. Well, we had a fair old fight with some of them and had to chase the others. A couple got away and we picked them up later. At the time, I was delighted and the Chief Constable has given a commendation to the beat man who saw the car, and put two and two together. That's the good news. The bad news is that the two who got away are pleading "not guilty" and that means that most of the shift is having to take time off when the case comes to court. That means changes of duty for people on other shifts, and so on. It's part of the job, but as a sergeant you have got to be careful about messing people about too often, when you have to get people to change shifts to maintain cover. They say the job comes first, but it's bad for morale.

'Police officers are like anyone else. There are good ones and not so good ones; the ones you have to chivvy a bit to get them to do the job properly, and the ones you know you can leave alone to get on with it. One man will turn up for work, full of a cold, and you have to force him to go home. Another will ring in and pretend to be at death's door, and you know there's nothing wrong with him. That's the one you have a few words with. If a man's bone idle, then he's certainly no good to the force. It's your job as a sergeant to find out what's wrong with him. Sometimes it can be domestic. I found out that one of the lads was in trouble because his wife couldn't manage the housekeeping. They had unpaid bills and that's not allowed in the police force. You have to keep out of debt. But with this lad, the inspector and I got him a loan from the force benevolent fund. We were able to pay off all his outstanding debts out of that, and now they are straight. Whilst he was having all this worry, he wasn't working properly. Now he's taking a new interest in the job.

'When things go wrong in this job, the first thing the bosses look for is the people who are to blame. And they want to know if the supervision has broken down. So, in a way, I'm held responsible if one of my shift drops a clanger. That keeps me on my toes. But you can't be constantly chasing your men and grumbling at them. We've all got to work together.

'I'm the first link in the chain of command. I have to work closely with the shift inspector. We spend a good part of each shift on supervision duties, and it's essential that if either of us is out of the station, the other knows where we are. When the inspector has a day off or is on leave, I have to assume his responsibilities as well,

Leadership

but when I'm "day off", then another shift sergeant takes over, and I do the same when the others are off. What happens is that each shift sergeant has an overall responsibility for a particular shift, but we have to work it amongst ourselves to ensure that there is one shift sergeant on duty all the time — although sometimes, even that isn't possible. It means that you are not with your own shift all the time, which is the ideal thing, but I find that working with another shift every now and again helps me to measure up my own performance. I see what the constables on the other shift are doing, and what they expect of their sergeant.

'I do feel in a position of responsibility towards my constables. Some of them are older than I am, but they don't resent me being in charge. If they did, I would soon tell them to cut it out. Everyone gets the same chance of promotion in this job. I rely on the older ones to get on with it. I know that they can't do the physical side of the job quite as well as they could 20 years ago, but you can't beat experience, and you certainly can't beat police experience. I respect them for what they know and I never ignore what they say. With the younger ones, especially the probationers, I like to think I can help to shape their careers. Sometimes we get a probationer who is just not up to the job. Then it's my task as the section sergeant to tell the inspector that the lad (or the girl) isn't going to make it. Sometimes you can say it's a borderline case, but you've got to be fair to the job and the other lads on the shift. We can't carry passengers and it's wrong to keep a youngster in the job when he could be just a uniform carrier for the next 30 years.

'I am usually the first one that the constables turn to when things have gone wrong. If a member of the public makes a complaint, the constable starts to worry about it, especially if he doesn't know about the complaints system. It's my job to help and advise him as much as I can. I try to find out his side of the story and tell him what to say in answer to the complaint. If it's a serious matter, then it depends if it's a case of internal discipline or not. If it is, I try to help by putting in a good word for him with the higher ups, but if he's let the job down, say it's a case of crime, then my first loyalty has to be to the service. The disciplinary aspect of being a sergeant is the hardest, but it's a responsibility that goes with the job, and if you dodge it once, then the constables know that you've done it, and you can never re-establish your authority.

'I have passed the examination to inspector and of course I

Leadership

would like to be promoted again. If I am, I reckon that what I have learned as a sergeant will make me a better inspector. The police system by which everyone comes up from the lowest rank is the right one. If we had people come in at, say, inspector level, like the army, then they would not get the co-operation or the respect from those under them. If you can't do the job yourself, or you haven't had the experience, you can't tell others how to do it.'

Inspector C was a graduate entrant. After taking his BSc degree he was selected from one of the places which this scheme offers each year. Under it, he served for two years as a constable on the beat in his Southern county force. During this time, he passed the qualifying examination for sergeant and then went to the Police Staff College at Bramshill, on the one-year "Special Course" designed to train promising young officers for the responsibilities of higher rank. This course is open to the graduate entrants, and to officers who have joined the service in the normal way. After Bramshill, Inspector C performed the duties of a sergeant in his own force for a year and was then promoted to the rank of inspector. He is now a unit inspector in a busy town which is also a seaside holiday resort.

'On my very first night on duty as a Patrol Inspector I got an emergency call. A train had crashed near a station on the outskirts of the town. I drove there straight away and was confronted with a twisted mass of wreckage, shocked people milling around, and the rescue efforts of the first people from the emergency services on the scene; the police, fire and ambulance services. All this was at the bottom of a thirty foot railway cutting. It was utter chaos, and for the first three quarters of an hour I was the senior police officer in charge of that incident with responsibility for bringing order out of chaos.

'My mind went back to the "Major incident" exercises we had at Bramshill. I knew my first jobs; the need to site the emergency services controls close to one another; communications to be established; a safe area for the personnel to rest; a mortuary team for the dead; a hospital documentation team for the injured; and a reception team to record details of the physically uninjured, most of whom were deeply shocked. All these things are needed to provide ready answers when people hearing of the accident ring police stations to enquire about relatives. In addition, there are a hundred and one small details which I either initiated or was involved in during that period.

'I spent much of that first forty-five minutes at the top of the Fire Brigade's Jacob's Ladder, looking down into the cutting where it was all taking place. I was not in any way involved in the rescue work. This was not my intention. I had to remain detached in order that I could supervise and assist in the co-ordinating of all the services which were present.

'I had also to detach a part of my mind from the immediate problems of the incident to remember that I was a unit inspector and as such I still had responsibility for the policing of an area of the town with over one hundred thousand people living in it. I had to ensure that the routine policing needs of that area were still being serviced as far as possible, with the extra demands of the emergency to cope with. This was a problem for a reason that might not be obvious to members of the public. When something like this happens, the natural reaction of every police officer is to want to be involved, to help as much as possible. My job was to make use of police assistance where it was needed, but to detail other staff to go on with their ordinary duties. I had to do this, too, in such a way as not to make them feel that their help was not wanted; that their other police work was just as important.

'My role is to lead a group of officers, numbering about 30 in all. I have to be able to assess the personalities of each and every one of these officers. I need to know what makes them tick and then to utilise this knowledge in order to weld them into an efficient working unit. I have to be able to pinpoint weaknesses, especially in officers with little service, and remedy these by training. They can only have so much training at district training centres and at force training schools. The remainder of their training is a matter for me, as their inspector, in consultation with the sergeants who are their immediate supervisors.

'I am the team leader and as such I am very conscious of the fact that I set the standards and my conduct and example will be subject to scrutiny. I must be seen to be consistent in my dealings with them and I have to stand in the middle ground between the supreme autocrat and the pliable democrat. It is obvious to all that there are occasions when emotions can run high — a colleague has been badly injured in a street fight, or a young child has been seriously

Leadership

assaulted. In these circumstances, I must ensure that my heart is always ruled by my head. It is important in such situations to display a calm, objective example to all the team present and, if necessary, to provide a restraining influence. I have emotions — but I must keep a tight rein on them so that justice as opposed to emotion prevails at all times and is seen to do so.

'The demands placed upon me are many and varied. I am the focal point for all matters of a welfare nature concerning my team, most matters of a disciplinary nature involving my team, and many of the prosecution decisions made in respect of work submitted by my team.

'I have a dual loyalty in that I must support and assist my subordinates, whilst providing complete loyalty to my senior officers. Whilst the desire to be popular can be tempting, it is respect I seek and this makes it impossible to run with the hare and hunt with the hounds. It is a precarious tightrope on which I must tread warily in order to achieve the right balance.

'I must be able to analyse situations which have occurred and extract from this analysis points which will assist me in the future. The Special Course was particularly valuable in this respect as it caused one to question all the time and to examine problems in the broadest possible context. This assisted me to discipline my mind to examine quickly, but critically, situations and make decisions, which I make in seconds but which Law Lords may ponder at their leisure. In the cold light of day I have to be able to justify these decisions, so I must be able to analyse and react quickly, but correctly.'

At present, the next rank above Inspector is Chief Inspector, but in most cases these officers simply act as deputies to Superintendents. There is now a growing body of opinion in the service that there is no longer a clearly definable role for the Chief Inspector as a separate rank, and the possibility is that it will be phased out in the near future.'

Detective Superintendent D is a deputy commander of the CID in a large provincial force. Superintendents perform widely varying roles in the service. He describes his job in this way:

'As a Detective Superintendent with four Sub-Divisions I am

Leadership

responsible to both my Divisional Commander and the CID Commander to organise the investigation of 15,000 crimes a year, to co-ordinate a staff of about 100 to produce the best results in detecting crime in my area, always bearing in mind that to the aggrieved citizen no crime is ever 'minor'.

'The best training one can have from my role is to have been through the ranks within the CID, to have the necessary understanding of the enormous pressures which fall upon all the departments, to have been to Detective Training Schools at constable and sergeant level, to attain the all important basic knowledge of the criminal law and procedures. Inspector and superintendent training complements this by providing extra and wider theory of management to put alongside experience.

'I have two seniors; the Divisional Commander and the CID Commander. It is imperative I keep both informed of daily events and provide them with early information of what is likely to fall into their lap at a later stage. Of course, I must not forget the Assistant Chief Constable (Operations), who may bypass them and enquire direct of me, asking for the "impossible — yesterday"!

'I must take responsibility for the actions of subordinates and therefore must know what they are doing. In the same vein I must not take from Detective Sergeants, Detective Inspectors and Chief Inspectors, their own responsibility at their levels. I must give them scope for decision making while holding the reins. An "Open door policy" on my part must always be best!

'If a decision is required and my advice is sought I must be seen to be decisive but at the same time receptive to others' views. At the end of the day I must make up my mind and give positive leadership so there is no doubt.

'In a serious crime, such as murder or armed robbery, I must take command, direct the enquiry in a proper manner, ensuring that correct lines are immediately followed, irrespective of the time of day, directing the right men to the task best fitted for them. The very mixture of personalities and background within the service is its strength.

'I must never let my emotions or thoughts influence my judgement or the judgement of my own men. The balance of justice at this time is with me. I have responsibilities to the aggrieved and the public at large. Injured parties and their relatives are to be comforted, witnesses will want to forget unpleasant happenings

Leadership

and leave the police station for the comfort of their homes and friends, I want them now to unfold the story.

'Suspects arrested must have quick attention, I must not forget the balance of justice for them. Should they be allowed to contact friends or solicitors? Will it interfere with "progress of the investigation or the administration of justice?" In the cold light of day will my decision made at that time satisfy the Court?

'Late one night a young German student walking with a group of German friends was followed by a number of youths and eventually stabbed to death. To deal with a dozen highly emotional and mainly young people who knew that their friend was alive one minute and is now dead, is difficult to say the least.

'They are unable to speak our language, what do we do? The phones are "red hot", vague details emerge slowly. Descriptions are piecemeal. The clock is ticking away. Every minute is vital. Experience has taught me that the first 24 hours in any enquiry are the most important. My men have already worked 12 hours or more, others are to be called out. An incident room has to be set up. Distraught German relatives are on the phone, "Is it my son who is dead?" A foreign national is involved; the diplomatic side must not be forgotten.

'Our friends in the media have heard a brief story, they want facts, details; how did he die? What weapon was used? Have you found it? The name of the deceased? Is it "student bashing"? I am not sure if the relatives of the deceased yet know, how much can I give them? I know I need the media. I want public help, but I must remember not to give all. Will it interfere with my enquiry or will it help? I must remember a possible Court hearing. Have I prejudiced the trial? It is all happening at once, have I been trained sufficiently? I hope so, but all the training in the world cannot cope with this real situation I have described. But certainly it helped!

'The CID must not be isolated, they must be part of the police team. Their uniformed colleagues are equally important. My task must be to encourage liaison at every level. I must give myself time to study crime trends and regularly be involved in talking to courses at Detective Training Schools and outside bodies who are always curious about our work.

'Liaison with other disciplines must also be part of my work, particularly in the sensitive area of non-accidental injuries to children. The Social Services are the key agency, saddled with this

Leadership

delicate task. Every battered baby is the victim of crime. Sometimes this is a difficult point to get over to social workers, who have been highly trained in theory, but some have little practical idea of "man's inhumanity to man". The balanced view must be put fairly at case conferences, but I must not forget my responsibilities "for the protection of life". The chief prosecuting solicitor, the Director of Public Prosecutions, senior pathologists have to be consulted, decisions as to whether to prosecute will have to be made in consultation with legal officers, ensuring always that we do not discriminate one against the other, and at all times are seen to be fair.

'I should be conscious of the need to look at reports of major frauds and have sufficient knowledge to assess details at an early stage to ensure that enquiries are made by specialists, and detectives are not left floundering. One must be able, at a later stage, to answer the inevitable queries that must come to the police because of the very nature of our work. Not everybody will be happy with any decision made. The CID must be projected in the right light to redress the balance portrayed by the media, and show the truth of what we are really like, surely one of my most important tasks. Staff can only do so much, they have families who need them. I must watch their natural enthusiasm which will keep them away from their families too long, too often. They will need rest, but I need them *now*.

'Finally I must ensure that our end product — the service we give to the public and which they demand — must be the very best. I must provide the leadership, but not like W S Gilbert's Duke of Plaza-Toro, in *The Gondoliers* who — "led his regiment from behind because he found it less exciting".'

Chief Superintendent E has been in the police service for twenty five years. He is now in command of a division of a large county force. This is what he says about his job:

'My primary responsibility as a Divisional Commander is to maximise the total efficiency of the Sub Divisions within my territorial command area by the co-ordination of resources at my disposal, the supply of advice and guidance to officers within the Division (particularly Sub-Divisional Commanders), and continuing supervision of procedures and systems in order to

Leadership

achieve a consistently efficient performance by all concerned — be they regular officers, members of the Special Constabulary or Civilian personnel, within the guide lines of force policy.

'To weld my Division into a competent, cohesive unit I need to be able to instruct and guide those under my command towards achieving a common purpose. By personal example I must set the standard required and by proper authoritative control ensure that my wishes are carried out. The right type of attitude adopted by police officers when dealing with members of the public is so important, and there is an obvious need to stress this aspect throughout the chain of authority from Divisional Command level. We are a disciplined organisation and I must make clear the standard required, which needs to be consistent and realistic, and do something positive about it, if officers do not attain it.

'Small rural communities, of course, experience different problems from those facing larger urban areas, and it follows that policing arrangements must be flexible enough to take these differences into account. Those Divisional Commanders with coloured minorities in the communities they police have a special responsibility to see that the total population is treated equally under the law, whilst at the same time recognising that the traditional police approach is perhaps no longer sufficient to meet special demands of this type. We must acknowledge that special problems exist and endeavour to forego closer links with the leaders and members of such minority groups to promote a reciprocal understanding. Police officers must never be put in a position where they fear, or are hesitant of, taking positive action to resolve a particular problem because of the colour of a person's skin. At the same time, however, it is our duty to do all we can to promote an understanding of our role within minority groups so as to prevent unnecessary escalation of minor events by ignorance or rumour.

'It is my responsibility to set the standard of efficiency within the Division, and I can only do this by taking a keen and active interest in the performance and welfare of my staff and their personal career planning and development. Of course staff appraisal is such an important management tool, and this responsibility rests with all supervisors. Any system of appraisal is absolutely worthless unless those involved in its operation are prepared to be totally honest and objective in their views.

Leadership

'I need to create the right environment to encourage Sub Divisional Commanders to come to me for support and advice when required without permanently seeking to use me as a prop. It is only by taking a critical and imaginative look at my staff and the police problems within my Divisional area, by conducting continuing reviews and appraisals of future strategic plans as well as existing procedures, that I can be satisfied that my Sub Divisions are not only operating efficiently now but will do so in the future.

'The emphasis of my job is to make the best use of my resources — nowadays, of course, this also means being cost conscious, and consequently demands are met in an order of priority. The facts are, quite simply, that we are too thinly spread on the ground and we are in constant danger of losing touch with our local community.

'In an emergency, people expect, and get, an instant response from police but we must have the manpower available to involve ourselves directly and consistently with the public. We are losing our traditional and very personal involvement and if this trend continues we may not be able to regain lost ground. All too often personnel from my Division have to be seconded for duty elsewhere to cope with political marches, meetings, football matches and expected large-scale public disorders at weekends and Bank Holidays. Of course, this cannot be avoided and these events must be properly policed, but in financial terms it is a most costly exercise and represents a further withdrawal of manpower resources from their local duties.

'What then are the qualities expected of a Divisional Commander by his Chief Constable? In my view he must:

— possess a sound operational background
— be able to accept the responsibility associated with decision making
— have a clear understanding of administrative and financial force procedures
— have the ability to manage his staff to get the very best out of them and ensure that they are doing their job well, also to interest and involve himself in their career development and experience
— be able to communicate at all levels — to be imaginative and possess flair.

Leadership
'Individuals will respond to effective and imaginative leadership. Careful career development will provide the useful experience needed to accept the responsibility of higher rank, but this really must be accompanied by sensible training if an officer is to be provided with the full range of ability required to cope with demands made on him within today's professional police service.

'Of course I work to an Assistant Chief Constable — in the main to ACC (Operations).

'The close working relationships that exist between a Divisional Commander and his Assistant Chief Constable (Operations) depends to a very large extent on mutual trust and professional respect. To my mind, he must be the type of person to be able to understand the operational problems I face. He should be prepared to assist me, when required, with advice and guidance and make available additional resources when they are needed to deal with specific policing problems. At the same time — if he has the right type of operational background and human qualities — he will appreciate that mistakes occur despite the most stringent safeguards.'

The Assistant Chief Constable in charge of police operations in a force is a major responsibility post, as Chief Superintentdent E has just pointed out above.

Mr F is another officer who joined the Metropolitan police twenty five years ago. He has attended three Bramshill staff college courses and transferred to his present force as a Superintendent. He was appointed as assistant chief constable in 1981 and is likely to become a chief constable in the near future. This is what he says about his present role:

'The role of an Assistant Chief Constable (Operations) is like so many senior management positions in that attempting to please all those who work to or above him, it is difficult to please everyone all the time. His primary role — that of providing advice to his Chief Constable on operational matters, and then carrying out his Chief Constable's policy in that sphere, is both demanding and rewarding. He must be a focal point to his Divisional Commanders, Detective Chief Superintendent and heads of traffic and Special Branch. He will be expected to leave them to carry out their roles with very considerable independence, and yet provide assistance when circumstances which are outside normal divisional resource levels occur. He should be ever ready to provide advice, and at the same time be willing to receive it, so that two-way communication flows easily.

'Matters of importance that demand his personal command vary from area to area, and will inevitably depend on the experience and ability of his Divisional Commanders, coupled with the outlook of his Chief Constable. As a general rule he should take personal command at siege or terrorist situations, large demonstrations where substantial aid has been called for from other Divisions, or other incidents, which albeit small in scale, are important in principle both to those concerned and the force — an example would be the non-accidental death of a serving officer.

'In the area of public order policing he will almost certainly have a mixture of experience within his Divisional Commanders, given that this type of experience is dictated by opportunity rather than rank or service, and a number of officers will arrive in the rank of Chief Superintendent with little or no experience of major demonstrations or processions. Whilst an ACC (Operations) will find it conforting to handle these situations by selecting over and over again those officers he knows to have the requisite experience, this will compound the lack of experience in others, and therefore a spread of these duties — even if some slight unease is felt by the officer in command — should be encouraged.

'There is a clear case for the Assistant Chief Constable (Operations) to be in touch not only with events in his own force and elsewhere in the United Kingdom, but also abroad. Acts of terrorism in Europe, the Middle East or further afield can lead to early repercussions in this country. In one way or another this can affect all forces, but it is particularly relevant to forces with an international airport, off-shore installations, or particularly sensitive persons or premises within their jurisdiction. The necessity, therefore, to be aware of current affairs across the whole ambit of the industrial, social and political scene is crucial to good police planning.

'It is clearly understandable in these difficult times of persistent crime and public disorder, that both the general public and the media should have an acute and sustained interest in police affairs. The operational team must do their bit to see that this interest is

Leadership

satisfied, and indeed to try and tap more effectively the very considerable reservoir of good will that exists for the police and the job they do. It is equally clear that chief officers will wish to demonstrate to police authorities that the public are getting the service they are entitled to expect, and they can only supply that assurance if they are kept clearly informed by their Assistant Chief Constables.

'Ideally an Assistant Chief Constable should have attended Senior Command Training. He should make the time to provide an input to his own force training. This is particularly important in respect of subjects like serious crime investigation, planning for demonstrations, or action at the scene of explosive devices where credibility is an important feature to the listener. Equally, an understanding of people, and in particular minority groups — racial or otherwise — is also an area which I believe calls for a greater input by those with the experience to contribute. This approach must be regarded as an integral part of our operational response, rather than as mandatory sociology lessons seen by many as far removed from the world of practical policing.'

The key figure in any provincial police force is the Deputy Chief Constable. In the Metropolitan Police, the Deputy Commissioner fulfils an almost identical role.

Mr G has been a policeman for more than thirty years. He joined a Midlands police force after serving in the RAF during his national service and, after attending the Senior Command Course at Bramshill he applied for his present post six years ago, when he was chosen by the police authority after they had interviewed four other candidates. This is his assessment of the role of the Deputy Chief Constable:

'The Deputy Chief Constable, more than any other officer in the force, including the Chief Constable, sets the tone of the force. He is the constant factor, whereas the Chief Constable has responsibilities outside the force and sometimes outside the force area. A modern Chief Constable has to operate as part of the local

Leadership

authority's corporate management team, even though he is not a local government officer as such. Finance is the name of the game nowadays, and the Chief spends a lot of his time fighting for the police force's share of the ratepayers' cake! He has to attend meetings of the police authority, meet the chairman of the police authority and the clerk to the police authority on many occasions, and be available to other council officials. On top of this, he often has to attend meetings at the Home Office, and he serves on important committees of the Association of Chief Police Officers. This means that he spends a lot of his time on official business out of the force area. When he is in the area, he tries to "fly the flag" for the force and accepts invitations from dozens of voluntary organisations to speak at their meetings. He is also a man who likes to get out and about and meet the members of his force.

'Fine. That's what the Chief Constable does, and I mention it so that it can be understood that the Deputy Chief Constable is very often, for much of the year, the Chief Constable! In his absence, I have to act for him, and as he carries the ultimate responsibility for what I do in his absence, I have to be sure that I am doing the right thing. The right thing, of course, is knowing what the Chief Constable would do in most given situations. Therefore, I have to enjoy not only a good personal relationship with the Chief Constable (and this is the third Chief Constable I have served under in a comparatively short time as deputy), I have to understand how he thinks as a policeman, as a commander, and as a strategist. The Chief Constable lays down the orders and decides the policy, but he relies on me as his Deputy and on his Assistant Chief Constables in charge of the departments of the force, to tell him what the situation is, and how we think it should be dealt with. There is a danger that Chief Constables, because they have so many high level responsibilities, will get too remote from what is happening on the ground. Some Chiefs, I am afraid, let themselves get bogged down with the paperwork and become more like managing directors than Chief Constables; it's all strategies and planning. The best Chiefs are the ones who know how to delegate responsibility whilst retaining effective control. The best deputies are those whom Chiefs can trust implicitly, and are able to give clear instructions and policy directives to those lower down the chain of command.

'That is how my job appears when I am, as it were, "looking upwards" — deputising for the Chief and acting as his eyes and

Leadership

ears of the force. The downward view is also important. I keep a general eye on what is happening in the departments, of course, but it is the job of the Assistant Chief Constables to run their own departments correctly. I will offer my opinion if I am asked for it. I will intervene only when I think something is beginning to go wrong, or where an Assistant Chief is away and a quick decision needs to be taken. Sometimes, of course, I have to act as an arbitrator between the competing claims on resources of the various departments. I chair the policy meetings at which we thrash out the budget details. It is up to me to see that as a managment team we all get on with each other. Of course there are sometimes personality clashes and I must not take sides between individuals. But I will not tolerate such differences spilling over to a point where they damage relationships between departments. That is rank bad management and poor leadership. So, just now and again, heads need to be knocked together and I do have a reputation for plain speaking.

'Further down the scale, the Deputy Chief Constable has a clear responsibility for discipline and also for welfare. I am the person who must decide whether an officer who has been complained against by a member of the public, or has been reported for an alleged breach of discipline by a senior officer, should be put on a discipline charge. In serious cases I have to tell the officer he is suspended from duty. But formal discipline is kept to a minimum. Often, all that is needed is a few well chosen words from an officer's Divisional Commander or the head of his department. I have to be careful on these occasions to make sure that the discipline aspect is not part of a wider welfare problem. Police officers are human beings, and nowadays we are getting more used to the idea of stress as a factor which affects the police, perhaps to a greater extent than people in other jobs would experience. I cannot be *au fait* with the family or personal circumstances of every member of the force, but I expect the commanders and supervisory officers to know if the people in their commands are experiencing problems, and I will not hesitate to reprimand a supervisory officer who should have been aware that something was wrong, and missed it.

'I make a point of seeing probationers during their service and doing what I can to encourage them. I study the staff appraisal reports by which senior officers assess our junior officers and this helps us when we are selecting men and women to be promoted. It is always nice to have people in my office and tell them that the Chief is going to promote them. It is much harder to tell someone that he has been passed over. This is especially difficult when the person concerned is holding middle management rank and has been banking on the next highest post. At times like that, I have to make sure that such an officer does not get bitter and to keep him motivated. It is not always possible, but I have to try, because an officer with rank who develops a grievance can be a problem for his subordinates as well as his superiors.

'I do not know a Deputy Chief Constable worth his salt who does not think that he does a more important job than his Chief Constable. That is not to say I would not have wanted to be a Chief Constable myself, but nowadays I am quite content to do a good job where I am. Moving to another force would be a major upheaval. Some years ago I read a book by a former Chief Constable who in his time was well known in the police service. He referred to one of his successors as "a good man, but always a number two, never a number one". Now I know that when this man was "number two" or Deputy Chief to the man who wrote the book, he was effectively the Chief Constable for months on end. It saddened me to think that a Chief Constable should be so dismissive of the loyal service of a colleague as to say something like that in print. I would think I had failed in my job if any Chief Constable I served did not think that I could have done the job of a Chief Constable.'

The men at the top

Finally, what of the men at the top, the Commissioner of Police of the Metropolis and the Chief Constables of the other forces, of whom there are 43 in England and Wales, nine in Scotland, and the Royal Ulster Constabulary? These are the men (so far no woman has been a serious candidate for the job of commanding a British police force) who are most in the public eye and carry a huge personal responsibility. When he was President of the United States of America, Harry S Truman had a little sign on his desk; *The buck stops here*. It is a reminder of the true situation which faces every chief of police.

Leadership
Commissioner of the Metropolitan Police

A Commissioner of the Metropolitan Police has an awesome responsibility. Besides commanding the largest police force in Britain, with the largest population to look after, the heaviest crime rate and the greatest concentration of inner city problems, the man in charge at New Scotland Yard has to take personal responsibility for the extra tasks which the Metropolitan calls its 'Imperial services'; duties and responsibilities which derive direct from the Crown and the central government, and he has to do this against a constant and unwavering glare of the media spotlight. The activities of the Metropolitan Police are newsworthy, not just in London, but to the whole country and throughout the world. When the force was embarrassed and shamed by the incident of the intruder in the Queen's bedroom, the Commissioner's personal responsibility for the safety of the Royal Family was brought home to him when the senior civil servant at the Home Office immediately asked him to resign. Sir David McNee refused, because it was not due to a failure of his policies or police security planning that the scandal occurred, but because the Palace authorities and, by implication, the Home Office, had been unco-operative when he had suggested much tighter security, and Sir David refused to be held personally accountable for the gross neglect of duty of junior police officers at the Palace. But if it could have been shown to have been Sir David's fault, then his would have been the head that rolled. There is a narrow dividing line between glorious success and abysmal failure and two other incidents involving the Royal Family show how great is the responsibility which the Commissioner shoulders. When an armed gunman tried to kidnap Princess Anne a few years ago, her police bodyguard was shot and wounded as he shielded her from the criminal. When, just before the Palace intruder incident, a man broke through the police lines as the Queen and her escort rode down the Mall to the Trooping the Colour ceremony, he was able to fire several revolver shots close to Her Majesty. Thankfully, these were blank cartridges.

Chief Constables

Similar heavy burdens of personal responsibility have to be accepted by the other Chief Constables. The Chief Constable of the

Leadership

Royal Ulster Constabulary commands a force which, since 1970, has seen nearly two hundred of its members assassinated by terrorists. For every police officer who has been murdered in the rest of the United Kingdom in this century, three have been slain in Northern Ireland since the present troubles began. It is not difficult to imagine the personal security problems which confront the Chief of the RUC and his immediate family, just as the Metropolitan Commissioner needs nowadays to have a bodyguard.

Provincial Chief Constables do not have to be concerned about their personal safety to anything like the same extent as the chiefs of police in London and Belfast, but their vulnerability when things go wrong has been demonstrated in recent years. The Chief Constables of Greater Manchester and Merseyside have had their battles with their local police authorities. Mr Kenneth Oxford faced strong pressure for his resignation when, at the height of the riots in the Toxteth area of Liverpool, the local police commander gave the order to police to fire tear gas into the crowd. Unfortunately, although this was the first occasion when the police had used tear gas against a rioting crowd in England, the canisters were unsuitable for use against crowds and some persons were quite seriously injured. Mr Oxford resisted demands for his resignation successfully, but he has had constant verbal battles with his police authority, which claims to be seeking greater 'accountability'.

At the height of riots which broke out in the Moss Side area of Manchester only a week later in 1981, the Police Commander there was under direct pressure from members of the police authority who were trying to persuade him to withdraw a strong police presence in the area. The Chief Constable, Mr James Anderton, was away in London but upon his return he launched a bitter attack on his police authority members, who are after all his employers, and this in turn led to strained relations and demands for his removal. Other Chief Constables have found their actions under serious challenge. The Chief Constable of Northumberland, Mr Stanley Bailey, faced local criticism over police action leading to the death of a man named Liddle Towers, even though an inquest exonerated the police. In 1982 the Chief Constable of West Yorkshire was sneered at in the press and strongly criticised by politicians when, following the arrest of the mass murderer known as 'The Yorkshire Ripper', it emerged that there had been very serious failures on the part of senior police officers. Mr Gregory

Leadership

bore overall responsibility for the operation, which assumed mammoth proportions and cost hundreds of thousands of pounds. With the wisdom of hindsight, critics were able to pinpoint glaring police errors, even to the extent of it being said that some of the killer's last victims need not have died. Mr Gregory, who had received glowing support from the Home Office and the Inspectorate of Constabulary when, before the arrest of the murderer, public impatience with the police performance had led to the calling of Scotland Yard, now had to face a retrospective review which concluded that the force had failed in many key areas. He angrily refuted all the criticisms, but he knew that there was a strong public demand that he should resign. At a more trivial level, the Chief Constable of Derbyshire was criticised by his police authority over expenditure on his personal office accommodation.

These are not easy times for chief officers. They used to be unchallenged, and apparently unchallengeable, autocrats. But we live in a society where authority is questioned all the time, and has to provide justification for its position. Chief officers are not officers of the local authority. They take their authority, as do all constables, directly from the Crown and they are personally accountable to the Law and to Parliament. The Police Act, incidentally, makes a Chief Constable personally liable for the wrongful acts (other than criminal acts) of any member of his police force. This is really a device to ensure that if a citizen with a justifiable claim for damages or compensation against the police, sues in court, he will recover any sums to which the court says he is entitled, but the provision in the Act serves to underline how the Law regards the personal responsibility of a Chief Constable for the manner in which he carries out the task of upholding the rule of Law in his police area.

A Chief Constable employs wide discretion over the operational policies pursued by his force, but he stands to be criticised if he appears to be acting in an autocratic, or even a controversial manner. For example, at Christmas 1983 the Chief Constables of Sussex and Nottinghamshire attracted adverse comment because they ordered their police traffic officers to conduct what amounted to a drive against drunken motorists. The law on drinking and driving does not allow the police to carry out 'random' checks on motorists to ascertain whether or not their alcohol content exceeds the legal maximum for drivers. The police must have seen a vehicle

Leadership

being driven erratically, or the driver must have been seen to commit a moving traffic offence, or have been involved in a road accident, before he can be required to take a breath test. But the police have the power to stop any motor vehicle on a road in order, for example, to test its mechanical efficiency, and whether it complies with all of the dozens and dozens of regulations which govern the construction of motor vehicles and their use on the roads. What happened in Nottinghamshire and Sussex was that under the guise of carrying out safety checks, the police were able to breathalyse thousands of motorists who had committed very technical offences (for which they were not prosecuted). The number of motorists actually caught driving with excess alcohol in their bloodstream was infinitesimal; only 77 out of over 4,000 tested in Nottinghamshire) but the campaign was justified by the Chief Constable on the grounds that lives were saved which would otherwise have been lost at a time of year notorious for road deaths and injuries brought about by alcohol. Some of the critics were not impressed. They thought that the chief officers, although they were not breaking the law, were manipulating it to carry out random breath tests which Parliament had forbidden.

More seriously, the cardinal issue in dispute at Brixton was whether the police commander was justified in using so many officers to carry out street stops and searches during 'Operation Swamp' against the perpetrators of street crime. No authority could be found by Lord Scarman (or anyone else) to say that police chiefs did not have the power to deploy their officers on such lawful duties as they decided. The Chief Constable (and the Commissioner) carries the sole responsibility for operational decisions, including those taken by his subordinate commanders.

The duty of the Chief Constable is to direct the police force under his command in the most efficient and effective manner of maintaining the rule of Law; the prevention and detection of crime, the prosecution of offenders against the Law, and above all, the protection of life and property. Under legislation due to be passed in the near future, chief officers are likely to lose a great deal of their powers to prosecute offenders because there is to be a system of local Crown prosecutors who will be responsible for prosecuting people charged by the police with criminal and other offences (this has always been the case in Scotland where the duty to prosecute lies with a local legal official called the Procurator Fiscal).

Leadership

How a Chief Constable sees his task, and the best ways of achieving his aims, is very much a question of personal preference. The Chief Constable of Devon and Cornwall for twelve years from 1970 was Mr John Alderson, whose faith in community policing was total. He had the personal authority to completely reorganise his force so that community policing became the central policy from which all else flowed. His police authority must have been similarly persuaded, because they after all held the financial purse strings and must have financed Mr Alderson's projects, but apart from the discipline of financial control, there was no way in which the police authority of Devon and Cornwall, had they been opposed to Mr Alderson's policies, could have instructed him to deploy his men on other forms of policing. The Law, in the shape of the courts, has greater power, as Mr Alderson discovered. Squatters were occupying land belonging to the local Electricity Board. Mr Alderson was asked by the Board to send officers to remove the trespassers, he refused because he felt it would harm police and public relations to do so. The Board went to the High Court, which ordered Mr Alderson to enforce the law, which required him to remove the trespassers.

Relations between the Chief Officer and the police authority are all important nowadays. A chief officer who does not get along with his authority, and cannot convince them that he is following the right operational policies, is going to find life difficult. And it is not just with the police authorities that the chief officer has to maintain good relations. He needs, obviously, to be well thought of in the community at large, and since the Police and Criminal Evidence Act has put a statutory duty on Chief Constables to consult local communities about their policing needs, chief officers have been obliged to pay much more attention to what the community leaders (and not necessarily the political leaders) are saying. The liaison committees set up under the Act are not given executive functions, but they are intended to assist Chief Constables, through their district and divisional commanders, to get the chief's policies across to the public, and to ensure that those policies are in line with what the public expects of the police in its area.

A Chief Constable is not only a commander, he is the team leader, and the wise chief will be good at communicating and listening. The worst kind of Chief Constable is the one who allows

Leadership

himself to be fully occupied with his office work and move almost exclusively in the administrative and political surroundings of county halls. This is bound to take up a lot of his time, but even in these days of large police forces a chief officer should get to know as many of his officers personally as he can, because he stands a far better chance of enlisting their support and co-operation if they know him as a human being and not just the name on the force notepaper, or the uniformed figure who turns up on ceremonial occasions.

Modern Chief Constables spend much time in the public eye, and it really is necessary nowadays for a chief officer (and for quite a lot of senior police officers) to learn the skills of communicating through the media. There is always a danger that a Chief Constable will become such a media personality that the public tends to lose sight of the unglamorous and confidential side of his work. There have been one or two well known Chief Constables who allowed themselves to be 'over exposed' on television and in the press. The media should not be used by chief officers for promoting their personal reputations, but for articulating police policies and making the public feel that the police do care about the job they are doing on behalf of the community.

It used to be said, and not at all truthfully, that every private soldier carried a field marshal's baton in his knapsack. With much more justification, the police service can say that every young constable starts off with an equal chance of one day being one of that small group of the service elite; the Chief Constables of Britain, or even the Commissioner of Police. No doubt young David McNee, the boy from a Glasgow tenement, never expected that one day he would be in charge of the Metropolitan Police, but he got there by virtue of his strength of character and his ability, first as a professional police officer and then as a police commander at lower levels of responsibility. Only a handful of the very best can get to the pinnacle of police success, but to be a commander of a British police force is a worthy ambition. It is a post which offers a person a remarkable opportunity to be of infinite service to the community.

Police powers

Sir Robert Mark, a former Commissioner of the Metropolitan Police, once said: 'A police officer in Britain has no real powers at all, save the power to inconvenience people'. It was a very perceptive remark because it pointed to a truth about British policing that is not often appreciated, especially by people living in this country: the powers which Parliament and the Law have bestowed on our police are the least of any country in the developed world.

Whenever 'police powers' are discussed, inevitably thoughts turn to crime and violence. The prevention and detection of crime; the control of traffic; and the duty to maintain public order; are the three areas of policing which could not be carried out unless the police had lawful powers over their fellow citizens. Through the centuries since the Barons forced King John to accept Magna Carta, the civil liberties of our citizens have been highly prized and protected. Only in wartime, for example, has Parliament been prepared to pass emergency legislation curtailing the liberties of the citizen, and even then the additional powers given to the police, the military, or to officials of Government have been carefully spelt out. One recent and regrettable exception to this general rule has come about because of the growing menace of terrorism on the British mainland. In the nineteen seventies, in the wake of bomb outrages in London and Birmingham which entailed much loss of life, Parliament passed The Prevention of Terrorism Act, which gave the police powers to detain people without charge for several days, and empowered the Home Secretary to remove certain people from the British mainland, or to issue orders excluding people from entering Britain. It was a mild enough measure by the standards of most countries faced with such a problem, but its passage through Parliament provoked an outcry; it is subject to constant review and opposition to extensions of the Act's provisions has grown stronger every year. Those who oppose the Act in Parliament are not any less opposed to the terrorists than the Government of the day; they simply argue that the continuation of the powers conferred by the Act are too great to be tolerated in a free society. Critics of the Act

Police powers

are also concerned that it discriminates against Irish people, and they say that in any case there is no proof that the Act is needed to counter the terrorist threat. Similar and stronger opposition is voiced against the emergency legislation in Northern Ireland itself, which has included powers of internment of citizens without trial, and still allows for people to be tried on very serious charges, including murder, by judges sitting without juries. The controversy surrounding these matters is mentioned here, not to point to conclusions one way or the other about the merits of the argument, but to emphasise how deep rooted in British society is the belief in the liberty of the subject and the need to restrict the powers of the police to an absolute minimum.

The Police and Criminal Evidence Act

In 1984 Parliament passed a most important piece of criminal legislation which has redefined the powers of the police in one comprehensive statute. This is The Police and Criminal Evidence Act. Before it was passed, the police had to cope with a confusing and bewildering situation in which they got some of their powers of arrest from the Common Law, which has grown up over the centuries, and others from Statute Law passed at different times to deal with different kinds of crime. The confusion was added to by the fact that some Acts gave the police powers of arrest for quite trivial offences, whilst others specified that certain actions were serious crimes, but omitted to give the police the power to arrest offenders unless they actually saw such crimes being committed, or had obtained arrest warrants. The Police and Criminal Evidence Act had the primary purpose, therefore, of simplifying and codifying police powers. But behind those comparatively innocent objectives, the guardians of our civil liberties — politicians and members of special interest pressure groups — saw in the Bill the biggest single threat ever to the civil liberties of the subject, and no major Act of criminal law legislation in modern times has ever encountered such fierce opposition. It is interesting, therefore, to examine what that fierce public argument was all about, because to understand the issue is to understand the nature of the relationship between the police and the British public.

The Government needed two attempts to get the Act through Parliament. The original Police and Criminal Evidence Bill was

Police powers

introduced at the beginning of 1983, and it ran into so much opposition that during its Committee Stage, when a Committee of Members of Parliament examined the Bill clause by clause and line by line, the Home Secretary had to accept more than three hundred amendments to its original provisions. Most of these were minor but some were fundamental. At the same time, there was an outcry from lawyers (including some judges); doctors, religious leaders, ethnic minority groups, and a host of others. Lord Salmon, a very distinguished Law Lord, said: 'I think that there is a danger that the Bill brings Britain closer to a police state.' A group of Church of England Bishops said: 'The Bill is so widely drawn and will rely so heavily on subjective interpretations that it could be misused.' Even right wing newspapers usually to be found amongst the strongest supporters of the police and 'law and order' had strong things to say. *The Daily Mail* said that the Bill 'was more likely to threaten traditional liberties than to protect society against the evil doer'. *The Sun* said: 'Powers so unlimited and so capable of being abused belong more properly to a police state.' The paper advised the Home Secretary to 'withdraw the whole misconceived, sinister measure'.

The Royal Commission on Criminal Procedure

In fact, the Bill followed a Report by the Royal Commission on Criminal Procedure, which had been set up by the previous (Labour) Government in the wake of public anxiety about the growth of serious crime in society. The Commission had been asked to examine, having regard both to the interests of the community in bringing offenders to justice and to the rights and liberties of persons suspected or accused of crime, whether changes were needed in the powers and duties of the police in respect of the investigation of criminal offences and the rights and duties of suspect and accused persons, including the means by which these were secured. The Commission was also asked to consider how people were prosecuted.

The Royal Commission sat for two years and heard evidence from many organisations ranging from the police to the civil liberties groups. When it reported, at the beginning of 1981, it said that the powers of the police to stop citizens and search for stolen goods should be extended throughout England and Wales. They

Police powers

found that the police in London had possessed such powers for a 150 years, and that police is some large provincial cities had similar powers, but elsewhere in the country the police had no legal power to stop and search, even if they had reasonable grounds for doing so. What was happening in practice, of course, was that the police in the areas where no statutory powers existed, were stopping and searching all the same, sometimes with the co-operation of the person concerned, but more often by using a mixture of bluff and persuasion. The Commission said that this was a nonsense, and they agreed with Sir David McNee, then the Commissioner, that it was wrong that police anywhere should have to operate without sensible and proper powers. Sir David, who began his career as a young constable in the toughest parts of Glasgow, told them: 'Many police officers have, early in their careers, learned to use methods bordering on trickery or stealth in their investigation' because Parliament had failed to provide them with the powers necessary to do their job properly.

The situation had, if anything, been made worse over the years by different Acts of Parliament which gave the police a power to stop and search for such things as illegal drugs and offensive weapons, but not for stolen property. The Royal Commission said that all these different powers should be replaced by a general power to all police to stop and search, on reasonable suspicion that the person they were stopping had committed, or was about to commit, a serious offence.

This was a straightforward, or a controversial, proposal, depending on whether it was looked at from the 'law and order' or the 'civil liberty' side of the argument. The Royal Commission was even more definite in its proposal that there should be one single power of arrest, and that all the different powers contained in dozens of Acts, and the anomalies between offences which carried a power of arrest and those which did not, should be swept away. The use of arrest, they said, should be governed by what they called 'the necessity principle'; an arrest should be made only where it was essential to achieve one of a specified list of purposes, for example, to stop an offence which was being committed or to prevent interference with witnesses or evidence. The Commission said that there should be a new power of arrest to enable the police to arrest people for offences, for which the penalties did not include imprisonment, in order to ascertain the correct name of the

Police powers

offender, where this could not be established at the time of an incident.

Another proposal made by the Royal Commission was that detention after arrest should continue only so long as it was necessary. They recommended regular reviews at intervals to see if it was still necesssary to detain a prisoner and that, except in relation to very serious charges, everyone who had been arrested would have to be released after 24 hours. For those it was necessary to keep in police cells for longer than 24 hours, the Commission said that the authority of a magistrates court would be needed. In the vast majority of cases, few problems would arise, just as few problems have ever arisen in the past, because people are charged with the offences for which the police have arrested them, and this charging procedure takes place as soon as they get to the police station, or as soon as possible afterwards. The problems crop up in the cases where people are detained in police cells but are not charged straight away. The Royal Commission said that it was time to do away with the old, probably unlawful phrase, that people were 'helping the police with their enquiries' when this really meant that they were arrested but not yet charged (and might never be charged before being released). So they proposed a new system of requiring that such persons who could not be released inside 24 hours should be put before magistrates to decide if their detention should continue, even if they had not been charged. The civil libertarians saw this as an infringement of freedom; others pointed out that there was in fact no absolute time limit on the length of time that the police could keep suspects in custody without charging them.

The Royal Commission's other recommendations contained some similarly controversial ideas, as well as proposals to strengthen the rights of suspects. In particular, they said that there should be Codes of Practice, which would be enforceable in law, governing such things as the searching, questioning and detention of suspects, and the manner in which they were treated at the police station. In general, however, these ideas disappointed those groups which had urged the Royal Commission that what was needed was less police power, not more. The Royal Commission made one important proposal which pleased the civil liberties interests. They said that the conduct of prosecutions should be taken out of police hands and be given to an independent prosecutions service.

Police powers
The Police and Criminal Evidence Bill

The outcry which greeted the Commission's report was nothing compared with the storm which broke when the Conservative Government published the Police and Criminal Evidence Bill. In some vital respects, the Bill went further than the Royal Commission. For example, it allowed the police, in some very unusual circumstances, to hold suspects up to 96 hours before they either had to charge them or let them go. Under the Bill (which is now the Act of Parliament that governs police powers) detention without charge is normally limited to a maximum of 24 hours; beyond then and up to 36 hours, the police will need the authority of a single magistrate to keep a prisoner in custody without charging him; and for up to the maximum of 96 hours, the authority of a full magistrates' court is needed. The Act makes it clear that before authorising such continued detention, the magistrates have to be satisfied that it is necessary and that the offence the police are enquiring into is a very serious one. In practice, this would mean something like a murder, or a gang robbery where one or two members of the gang had been caught or were being questioned, and their accomplices were still at large. The Act lays it down that people who have been arrested should be granted access to a lawyer if they are not going to be released once they have been charged, but such access can be withheld for up to a maximum of 36 hours if the police have good grounds for believing it would hamper them in their inquiries into serious charges.

As a result of the Act, the police throughout the country do have the power to stop and search people for offensive weapons, house breaking implements and other articles used in connection with theft. The police must act on reasonable suspicion that the person they stop and search has committed an offence for which he could be arrested, or is about to commit one. What is new about this power, apart from the fact that it applies throughout England and Wales (Scotland has different laws), is that for the first time the police must now, by the terms of this Act, identify themselves as police officers (they could be in plain clothes). A police officer carrying out a stop or a search is obliged under the Act to make a written record of the search either on the spot, or as soon as possible afterwards, and the person who has been stopped has a right to demand a copy of that record. The Act says that a police

Police powers

officer who is searching someone in the street can only ask that person to remove an outer coat, jacket or gloves.

This general power to stop and search was attacked by the civil liberties groups and politicians who argued that it would be used more against young black people in inner city areas than anywhere else. There were also protests about provisions in the Act which allow the police to search the homes of people who have been arrested for serious crimes, to set up road blocks in high crime areas (it was suggested that this would allow the police to cordon off an entire neighbourhood and then carry out mass searches of the population!).

But it was not only the pressure groups normally suspicious or hostile towards police powers which protested about the Police and Criminal Evidence Bill when it first came out. The doctors, churchmen, lawyers and journalists were very upset about proposals which would have allowed the police, in certain circumstances, to demand access to confidential records. The Government was taken by surprise at the very strong opposition it encountered to these proposals, but once again, the public was demonstrating its strong commitment to civil liberty and opposition to the encroachment of the state into the private life of the citizen. As a result of all the criticism it received, the Government was forced to accept major changes to the Bill, including having to guarantee that the police would not be able to demand access to confidential legal, medical and similar records. More than 300 amendments had been made to the original Bill when Parliament was dissolved in 1983 before it had been passed into law. When the Bill was republished after the General Election, it embodied all the concessions and changes that had been made and, now it is the law, it is the main 'working tool' of police officers who are in any way engaged in the investigation of crime; detectives and uniformed police alike.

So the young police officer soon learns that the donning of a police constable's uniform, and the taking of an Oath of Office, does not place him in a position of unchallenged or unchallengeable power over his fellow citizens. Just the opposite. The exercise of his powers is governed by the Police and Criminal Evidence Act and the Codes of Practice made under it. Any breach of those codes renders the police officer liable to disciplinary action. The British police service was unique amongst the police forces of the world in having enshrined its disciplinary system, and the arrangements for

Police powers

dealing with complaints against the police from members of the public, in an Act of Parliament, some Commonwealth police forces now have similar Acts of their Parliaments.

Police discipline

The police is a disciplined service, of course, and as such it must have a system of discipline to enforce the rules of the service. But apart from this internal discipline, the police are also subject to disciplinary action if it is decided that they have acted improperly in their dealings with members of the public.

Every year, about thirty thousand complaints are made against the police by members of the public. If this sounds a lot, it has to be kept in perspective. There are more than 120,000 police officers in England and Wales, and every police officer performs over two hundred days of duty every year, so altogether police officers undertake more than 25 million tours of duty a year. Looked at in this way, a ratio of one complaint to every 800 days of police duty is very small, and it is even smaller when, as is the case, it transpires that the vast majority of complaints do not justify disciplinary actions against the police officer concerned. It might be thought surprising, therefore, that over the past 30 years, the question of complaints against the police has attracted so much public attention. The Royal Commission on the Police was set up at the end of 1960 in the wake of a series of cases of misconduct by the police which caused public anxiety. This Commission set up a new framework, which was included in the Police Act of 1964, which required that all complaints should be recorded and properly investigated. Where a complaint alleged that a policeman had committed a crime (or even suggested the possibility of one) the report of the investigation of the complaint had to be sent to the Director of Public Prosecutions, who deals with all serious prosecutions on behalf of the Crown. It is therefore, the Director of Public Prosecutions, and not the police themselves, who decide if a police officer should be charged with a criminal offence. The Royal Commission also said that outside London, it was the duty of the police authorities to satisfy themselves that complaints, in the forces for which they were responsible, were dealt with in the proper way.

The system set up by the Police Act 1964 still failed to satisfy the

Police powers

critics, and public anxiety was further aroused by the revelations, in the early seventies, of widespread corruption affecting members of the Metropolitan Police Criminal Investigation Department. The result of further public debate was the setting up, in 1976 of an independent complaints board to decide whether or not complaints against the police were justified. This system soon attracted more criticism and none of the systems which have been tried has met the major point of the critics; that the actual investigation of complaints against the police is carried out by police officers. The Police and Criminal Evidence Act, whilst setting up a new Police Complaints Authority with powers to supervise investigations whilst they are taking place, and to satisfy itself that such investigations are genuine enquiries into the truth of what took place, still leaves the actual work of investigating a complaint in the hands of the police themselves, and so it is doubtful if the critics are going to be any more satisfied with the changes introduced by the Act, than they were with previous attempts to find a satisfactory way of ensuring that complaints were fully and fairly enquired into.

In that very small minority of complaints cases where it is decided that disciplinary action should be taken against a police officer, and in a rather larger number of cases where members of the public are not involved, but a police officer's superiors allege he has committed a breach of discipline, the Police Discipline Regulations and the Discipline Code provide the framework under which such matters are dealt with. A policeman who is found guilty of a breach of discipline by his Chief Constable or by a discipline board of senior officers in the Metropolitan Police, can be punished by a wide range of sanctions, ranging from a caution or a reprimand to a heavy fine, demotion in rank, or dismissal from the force. Despite what the critics say, the police service attaches major importance to its reputation for integrity, and the police officer who lets down himself and the service can expect to be dealt with severely.

Police accountability

This question of complaints and discipline goes to the major issue of public concern affecting the police service today; its accountability. In fact, this argument has been central to the relationship between the police and society ever since the

Police powers

professional police were established in 1829. This is why the Police and Criminal Evidence Act is regarded by many people as establishing a new and dangerous framework of additional powers for individual police officers (and it is also why many police officers would argue that, on the contrary, the Police and Criminal Evidence Act has established so many safeguards for the suspect that it is going to be all the more difficult for the police to mount an effective response to the growth of crime in society).

Who controls the police and ensures that they remain the servants of the people, and never their masters? We have this unique division of responsibility between central and local Government. The Home Secretary is the Minister responsible to Parliament for police actions, and in the Metropolitan Police District he is also the police authority for that force. Every other police force has a police authority and, as explained earlier, these have statutory duties to provide and maintain an adequate and efficient police force in their areas. But both the Home Secretary and the police authorities are charged with the responsibility for ensuring that the police are accountable for their actions.

But what do we mean by 'accountability'? Who makes the decisions in police forces which affect the way the force and its individual members go about the job of policing? To a very large extent, it is the Commissioner of Police or the Chief Constables, not the police authorities made up of elected councillors and local magistrates, and this absence of genuine executive powers of the police authorities (or even the Home Secretary) has led in recent years to calls for more 'democratic' control of the police, and for chief officers to be subject to directions as to the policies they carry out. One of the problems which Lord Scarman identified, in his report on the 1981 Brixton disturbances, was the breakdown in relationships between the local authority in Lambeth and the local police commanders. Scarman recommended that there should be a system of police and local authority consultation in London and since then a network of borough police liaison committees has been established. This has been followed through in the provinces also, but these consultative committees do not have any powers; they are purely forums for discussion at which the police can tell local councillors and community leaders what they are doing; and the community representatives can say what they expect of their police. It is hoped in this way that good relations between the police

Police powers

and the public can be maintained, based on common understanding of what each wants of the other; the public want the police to protect them; the police want the public to co-operate with them to protect lives and property, and to prevent and detect crime.

The police, and chief officers especially, maintain that democratic accountability and control of the police must not include the right of politicians, either local or national, to give orders to the police on what are regarded as operational matters. They say that only Parliament and the Law can be supreme in these matters. The Home Secretary (of any party) will always say that he is not in a position to give orders to the Commissioner of Police or Chief Constables about operational matters (and certainly not as to which crimes to investigate or to prosecute). The Home Secretary can and does issue 'guidance' to Chief Constables, but that is what it is, not orders which must be obeyed. Such control as he has over police forces lies in a number of powers conferred on the Home Secretary under the Police Act. The most important of these is the power to approve the appointment of the Chief Constable and other Chief Officer ranks above Chief Superintendent. The Home Secretary can require a police authority to retire a Chief Constable in the interests of the efficiency of the force, which is a reserve power for getting rid of a Chief Consteable who is obviously incompetent or unfit in other ways for the job. And the Home Secretary can call for reports from chief officers on any matters affecting a police force. He has the power to set up a special inquiry into any matter affecting a police force. His ultimate power of sanction lies in the power to withhold the Home Office contribution to police expenditure. This power has not been used since before the last war, but all expenditure incurred by police authorities needs to be approved by the Home Office, and police authorities cannot afford to ignore what the Home Office says on expenditure. The Government pays for more than half the cost of the police.

The Home Secretary decides what is the appropriate size of a police force. This is arrived at by consultation between the Home Office, the Inspectorate of Constabulary, and the Chief Constable. The figure arrived at is known as the authorised establishment of the force, and it is a very important decision. Eighty per cent of the cost of the police service is accounted for by the pay, allowances and pensions of the police. As police pay has dramatically

Police powers

improved, and the size of the service has grown, the total cost of the police service has more than doubled in the decade of the seventies, so that currently it is more than £2 billion annually. This is one of the reasons, incidentally, why there is now so much effort being made in police forces to use civilians on jobs that do not really require the experience or powers of a policeman — civilians are much cheaper to employ!

The Home Secretary has rather more power of control and direction of the police service as a whole than he does over individual police forces. It is he who makes the Police Regulations which govern the way the service is organised, and such things as the pay, allowances and working conditions of the police; the qualifications for recruitment and promotion of police officers; the retirement of police officers; the maintenance of discipline (the Discipline Regulations); the duties which police may be engaged on; the uniforms and equipment of the police, and similar things. The Home Secretary lays the regulations before Parliament for approval, after he has consulted a body called the *Police Advisory Board*, which consists of representatives of the police staff associations and the police authorities. This looks after the professional subjects covered by the regulations, such as recruitment and training, promotion and discipline. The *Police Negotiating Board* deals with police pay and pensions and conditions of service, and here the Home Secretary has the power to approve or disapprove agreements on such matters reached by the Negotiating Board.

If the Home Secretary has surprisingly few powers over individual Chief Constables, however, the police authorities which are nominally in control of police forces have even less. One of the incidents which led to the appointment of the Royal Commission on the Police in 1960 was a disagreement between the then Chief Constable of the Nottingham City Police and the police authority. They wanted a report from him concerning police inquiries into an alleged crime. He refused to supply the information, saying that it was not a matter for the police authority, and the authority responded by suspending him. The Home Secretary intervened swiftly, upholding the stand taken by the Chief Constable, and he was reinstated, but the incident caused a great deal of ill feeling and other local authorities made it clear that they were dissatisfied with the legal position between themselves and their Chief Constables.

Police powers

Since the Police Act, the complaint of police authorities has been that they have been saddled with responsibilities for maintaining adequate and efficient police forces, and for ensuring that complaints are properly dealt with, but have been denied the means of doing it. For example, every police force in the country, except the Metropolitan Police, is inspected every year by one of Her Majesty's Inspectors of Constabulary. They prepare a detailed report for the Home Secretary on the way the police force is being conducted, and they will draw his attention to any particular problems or deficiencies they have encountered during their inspections. Yet that report, which amounts to a professional assessment of whether or not the force is indeed 'adequate and efficient' is a confidential document and neither the Chief Constable nor the police authority see a copy of it. Of course, as a matter of courtesy, the Inspector of Constabulary meets members of the police authority during his inspection and will discuss matters with them, but he does not reveal the contents of his report. An example of how frustrating this can be occurred after the notorious 'Yorkshire Ripper' case, in which a man murdered a number of women and was not captured for many months. There was very serious criticism of the way in which the West Yorkshire police had conducted the inquiry, and the Home Secretary appointed an Inspector of Constabulary to conduct an investigation of the case. His report was understood to be severely critical of the force and as a result changes were made to existing arrangments for setting up such major inquiries. Senior officers in charge of the investigation were criticised, and it was stated that some senior officers involved would not be promoted in the future. Neither the Chief Constable, who attracted the brunt of the criticism, nor the police authority, was permitted to see the full report. All they saw was what was contained in the statement made by the Home Secretary in Parliament.

The argument about police powers, accountability and efficiency is likely to go on for a long time ahead. The principle of local control, working in harness with central government, is generally accepted, but it is the practice which gives rise to problems. There is a lot of anxiety in police circles because the Labour Party, which tends to be in the majority in the police authorities which govern the urban police forces, has declared that a future Labour government would give local councils far more say in the control of

Police powers

the police, including the establishment of a police authority for London. The Party's proposals for the police in London were set out in the manifesto for the Greater London Council (GLC) election in 1981. It was made clear that such a police authority would determine police priorities and appoint and promote senior police officers. Amongst the pledges made by the Party were the abolition of the Special Patrol Group and the Special Branch.

Of course, ordinary police officers tend to view arguments about the accountability of police forces and the relationship between Chief Constables and police authorities as something which hardly concerns them as they go about their daily duties. But then incidents occur which show how close these questions are to direct political (or 'democratic', as some prefer to call it) control of the actions of individual officers in specific cases. In Greater Manchester at the time of the 1981 disturbances, there were extraordinary confrontations between senior police officers and members of the police authority when the problems in the Moss Side district were at their height, with the vice chairman of the police authority seeking to persuade the Police Commander to withdraw police contingents from the area; in Merseyside during and after the Toxteth riots, there was similar tension and disagreement between the police authority and the Chief Constable, especially when for the first time ever a police force used tear gas to quell a riot; and more recently in the West Midlands the police authority demanded reports from the Chief Constable after a series of incidents in which it was alleged that police had broken into the homes of innocent citizens and made wrongful searches. The police authority, after considering the report of the Chief Constable, which tended to exonerate his officers, divided on party political lines and decided to censure the Chief Constable and the officers concerned.

These incidents, involving as they do the three largest police forces outside London, suggest that the argument about political control of the police is not going to go away in a hurry.

Other police units

The Dog Section

All police forces have dog sections and from soon after the First World War, when the ways in which dogs could assist the police were first appreciated, the contribution they have made to police operations has increased rapidly.

At first, police officers were simply given permission to take their dogs out with them on their foot patrols, but then the forces began to accept gifts of dogs, usually German Shepherds (Alsatians), and started to train them for police work. In the early years, bloodhounds were used to follow scents but it was soon found that these dogs lacked the hardiness and stamina required for police work, and their tracking skills are not as good as several other breeds now in use with the police. By far the most numerous of these is the Alsatian.

Most police dogs nowadays have been carefully bred by the police dog sections. Some dogs are accepted for training, but the police prefer to breed their own animals because temperament is all important.

Officers may volunteer for the dog section after completing their probationary period. They are selected on the basis of their understanding of animals, and dogs in particular, and their own aptitude. Just like their animal charges, dog handlers have to be able to work as part of a man/dog team, and there are other requirements of belonging to the section which are not obvious at first sight. Dog handlers have sole charge of their animals. The dogs live in their homes and the handlers must devote part of each day to exercising and grooming their charges.

The dogs, before being accepted for permanent work with the section, have to satisfy the training instructors that they are fully obedient and absolutely trustworthy. They must, of course, be up to peak fitness and their courage must be unquestionable. A dog handler must be prepared for the disappointment of going through a lengthy training course with a young animal, only for it to be rejected as unsuitable for the work. Then the dog, of which he and his family may have become fond, has to be taken away and the

Other police units

handler has to start all over again with another animal.

Different breeds are suitable for different kinds of police work. Alsatians are invaluable as guard dogs, trackers, and for normal dog patrol work. Labradors have a highly developed sense of smell which enables them to be trained for detecting drugs, and in recent years, explosives. Other breeds, including Dobermans, Rottweilers and Boxers have been tried over the years, but not with any great success.

A dog handler must expect a great deal of dislocation of his private life because the police may have need of a dog's assistance at any time of the day or night. It is work which often requires the dog and the handler to be out in all weathers and in exposed locations. Perhaps the search may be for a missing child, an escaped criminal, or a consignment of illegal drugs. At other times, the handler and his dog may be needed to break up a fighting mob, or to act as a deterrent when large groups of potential troublemakers are in the streets, such as when a major football match is taking place.

Some officers, once they have made the choice and been accepted, are content to spend their whole careers in the dog section. This entails some sacrifice, because obviously in such a relatively small section, career opportunities are strictly limited. Others find a few years in the Section an invaluable experience which stands them in good stead when they move on to other departments.

Underwater Search Units

Police underwater search units consist entirely of volunteers from the force. The officers who belong to the units are not full time, they spend part of their time on training but are otherwise called out for specific tasks. The work can often be extremely dangerous and unpleasant, involving searches for dead bodies in rivers, canals and ponds. Divers are often called in to search for abandoned stolen goods and so on.

Mountain Rescue Teams

In forces with mountainous areas within their boundaries, police mountain rescue teams are indispensible. Their members are all

Other police units

volunteers and become extremely expert in locating and rescuing climbers in difficulties. Their work involves considerable risk, because the bulk of calls for their help comes at times when the teams are likely to face appalling weather conditions. The police units work in close co-operation with other rescue teams.

Police horses

Nowadays, fewer forces have mounted sections but those that have find that police horses are still as popular as ever with members of the general public. It is to be acknowledged that, except in dealing with crowds, the usefulness of police horses has declined over the years and their modern role, apart from crowd control, is largely ceremonial. Recently, the use of police horses to deal with disorder at industrial disputes has been shown to be effective, but controversial. Here again, because the sections have become so small, career prospects are limited and officers seeking promotion have to move out into other departments.

River Police

The Thames Division of the Metropolitan Police proudly asserts that it is older than the force itself, and it is true that there were professional police officers patrolling the River Thames in boats some decades before the Metropolitan force was founded. In those days, officers of the River Police were armed with cutlasses, which came in very useful when dealing with the cut-throats and thieves who operated in what was then a busy port and on the seedy waterfront described so vividly by Dickens and other historical writers.

As the Port of London has declined so swiftly since the war years, so the work and the size of the Thames Division has been reduced, but the force still maintains regular patrols of the reaches of the river within the Metropolitan Police District, and maintains a number of floating police stations from which the familiar police launches operate. The river still has a lot of commercial traffic and the force is responsible for maintaining safety on the waterway.

Members of the Thames Division tend to be river police officers first and always, sacrificing the greater career opportunities they

Other police units

would find in other Departments for the satisfaction of taking part in the highly specialised work of the Division.

Most other forces with large waterways or stretches of coastline maintain waterborne departments.

Police Helicopter Units

The helicopter is just beginning to make an impact in this country, whereas it has become standard to most American forces and is widely used in the police forces of many other countries. One of the major reasons why helicopters have not made much progress with the British police is the high cost of the machines and the expense of operating them. Only the Metropolitan Police has been able to purchase its own machines, and by 1984 three dual engined machines were operating from the Section based at Lippits Hill in Essex.

So far, the police have not had their own officers trained as helicopter pilots, preferring to use qualified personnel who are employed, either by the force or on contract with a private company.

Several forces have found it valuable to hire private helicopters to assist in police searches of wide expanses of open countryside, or in the mountainous areas, for missing persons. Here, cost is the inhibiting factor, another difficulty is the strict regulation and restrictions imposed by the aviation authorities on the use of these machines. It is unlikely, therefore, that the British police will ever match their American and Continental counterparts in their widespread use of helicopters.

The 'other' forces

In addition to the 43 police forces in England and Wales, the nine in Scotland, and the Royal Ulster Constabulary, there are a number of 'other' police forces which do not come under the control of the Home Department.

British Transport Police

The largest of what are called the 'non-Home Office' forces is the British Transport Police, sometimes mistakenly called the Railway Police. Before the transport industry was nationalised after World War II, the private railway companies and the port owners maintained their own police forces. These were combined into one force, which is now just over 2,000 strong. In addition to policing the property owned by British Rail and the Docks Board, Transport Police are responsible for London Transport. It is a national force which means that its members can be required to serve anywhere in the country.

The British Transport Police is run on exactly the same basis as the other forces. Its members have jurisdiction on all property belonging to the British Railways Board and the Docks Board and London Transport, and this extends to inquiries elsewhere arising from incidents on such property. Transport Police are now trained at the Police District Training Centres. Naturally, in addition to such training they require a detailed knowledge of the law affecting transport and the various bye-laws and regulations which specially apply to them.

Ministry of Defence Police

This force is an amalgam of the separate constabularies which were maintained by the three services before they were combined into the one Government ministry. Its members have jurisdiction on Ministry of Defence property only. Although Ministry of Defence police are paid the same rates and enjoy similar service conditions of other police forces, they do not undertake the same range of

Other police units

duties, being mainly concerned with the security of access to defence establishments. Recent years have seen drastic cut backs in the scope and size of this force and frankly, as a career it can only be recommended in cases where efforts to join other forces have failed.

Royal Parks Police

As the name implies, this force is responsible for the policing of the Royal Parks. Although its members are paid only slightly less than their counterparts in the regular force, again it cannot be said that they perform anything like the same range of duties.

Docks Police

A number of port authorities, notably the Port of London Authority and Merseyside, maintain their own police forces. These have been run down in recent years along with the port industry generally.

Atomic Energy Authority

The United Kingdom Atomic Energy Authority maintains a constabulary whose primary duty is the protection and security of the Authority's highly sensitive establishments all over the country. Its members also provide escorts when sensitive atomic material is being conveyed between such establishments.

The Armed Services

Quite a number of present day police officers began their police careers in the armed forces, serving in one or other of the police corps maintained by each service.

The Army

The Corps of Royal Military Police is responsible for policing the Army in the United Kingdom and abroad. Its role may be summarised (as in the case of the police corps of the other services) as:

Other police units
(a) the provision of general garrison police facilities
(b) law enforcement and crime prevention
(c) tactical police support (eg motorised escorts) in all phases of military operations.

With British troops and their families and employees (who are British citizens) abroad, the military police have jurisdiction subject to agreements between Britain and the host country. In addition to a working knowledge of the criminal law of our own land and the country in which our troops serve, military police have to ensure that the Regulations governing the internal discipline of the Army are obeyed.

The other military police corps are:

The Royal Navy Regulating Branch
The Royal Marines Police
The Royal Air Force Police

Details about these military police corps can be obtained from any recruiting office. They offer either a complete career or, as mentioned above, a useful introduction to police work for young people who wish to combine their ambition to be police officers with a wish to serve for a shorter time in the armed forces. It should be noted, also, that Chief Constables of 'civil' police forces are able to accept suitable applicants from the armed forces who are above the maximum recruiting age. Preference is likely to be given in such cases to former military personnel with police experience.

Civilians in the police

For a service which has always taken pride in not being a military organisation, it is odd that the police should always refer to their colleagues who are not police officers, but work alongside them, as 'civilians'. And there are now something like sixty thousand 'civilians' working in the police forces of this country. What is more, this rough ratio of one civilian to every two police officers is going to grow over the next few years, for a variety of reasons.

Not everyone who wants to, can become a police officer, but working in the police service as a civilian employee can often offer similar job satisfaction and quite a lot of the people who are doing this today, chose their work as the 'next best thing'. On the other hand, it would be wrong to regard all, or even most, civilian employees, as 'disappointed coppers'. Of course, they are nothing of the kind, and the work they do is vital to the good performance of the police forces they work in. Indeed, young people who are attracted to the idea of working with the police, would nowadays be well advised to look at the role of civilians and see whether the particular jobs that they perform, might not be more suitable for them. Someone who wants to work with computers, for example, might find very good career opportunities working in a police force with computers, rather than becoming a police officer and finding that only rarely will he have the chance to work with computers. Again, a young person with a great interest in forensic science would be well advised to look at the chances of employment, once he has obtained the necessary academic qualifications, in the Home Office forensic science laboratories. Home Office pathologists are indispensible to the police in investigating all manner of sudden deaths, and of course some of them, such as the late Sir Bernard Spilsbury and Professor Francis Camps, became better known to the public than even the most celebrated senior detectives in Scotland Yard's murder squad. That was in the days when a man's life literally hung upon what the Home Office pathologist said about the significance of a thread of cotton found at a murder scene. If nowadays the morbid sensationalism of murder trials has gone, along with capital punishment, the public tends to lose sight

Civilians in the police

of the importance of pathologists and forensic scientists. Yet it is they, much more than the police investigators, whose evidence is so often conclusive in deciding the guilt or innocence of people accused of serious crimes. This is never better illustrated than in the recent scandal involving a Home Office forensic scientist whose evidence led to the conviction of a man charged with murder, who served several years in prison before he was released. It was established that the forensic scientist had given unsatisfactory evidence and, as a result, enquiries were re-opened into a number of other cases in which he had been involved and several people convicted were either freed on appeal or pardoned. Against this, forensic evidence has determined the result of many cases by convicting criminals who would otherwise have escaped justice, and of course forensic scientists, during police investigations, must have enabled the police to eliminate many innocent people from their enquiries.

Scenes of Crimes Officers

Scenes of Crimes Officers are the 'technicians' of forensic investigation of crimes. Until recently, police officers were used for this work, but the posts have been 'civilianised' as part of the general policy of not employing trained and experienced (and expensive!) police officers on duties which do not require police powers, experience or training. Scenes of Crimes Officers, as the job title suggests, visit the locations of crimes and look for scientific evidence; fingerprints, bloodstains, footprints, and anything which might provide a scientific clue to assist the police. For example, a cigarette butt would be taken by a Scenes of Crimes Officer for subsequent examination in a forensic science laboratory. It is just possible that a scientist, by examining the saliva traces or lipstick remains on the butt, could give the police an important lead as to the identity of the person who had smoked that cigarette at the scene of the crime; that, for instance, he had a very rare blood group.

Fingerprints

Fingerprints are unique aids to crime investigation (and often to the identification of dead bodies). The science of fingerprinting is a very exact discipline, based upon the claim that no two fingerprints will ever reveal exactly the same pattern of 'loops' or 'whorls' made by the skin on the tip of a finger. It is a remarkable fact that, when this claim was first made by the pioneers of fingerprints at the turn of the century; people like Sir Edward Henry, for many years Commissioner of the Metropolitan Police, it was treated with great scepticism by the courts. But as the numbers of fingerprints on police files all over the world have grown into countless billions, the 'impossible' has never happened; the discovery of two people with an identical fingerprint. New techniques have enabled fingerprints to be obtained from surfaces which once defied the known processes. The use of computers has replaced a great deal of the manual indexing and storing of fingerprints, and has enabled comparisons between prints on files and those taken from suspects to be made with startling speed; minutes instead of days. And the computer techniques have gone a long way to eliminate the one possible flaw in the otherwise foolproof system of fingerprint evidence; human error by the expert making the comparison. Incidentally, the criminal courts require that only fingerprint officers of several years standing may give evidence in court as to the results of fingerprint analysis. On the other hand, Scenes of Crimes Officers often have to appear in court to testify as to how they came to find an item of evidence which has become an exhibit in a criminal trial.

Police photographers

One highly specialised and fascinating aspect of police civilian employment is the photographic department. Police civilian photographers are crucial to their role as recorders of vital information as soon as possible. It could be that a police photographer is called to the scene of a murder to capture the scene as it was discovered by the police, before the body of the victim is disturbed in any way; or to the scene of a serious road accident. Photographers for the police develop very special skills indeed, learning how to get good pictures of fingerprints on objects, for example. They also are frequently required to produce their photographs in court, and give evidence of the circumstances in which they were taken. Nowadays, police photographers may also be skilled in the techniques of filming of crimes, etc.

Civilians in the police
Computer operators

The much increased use of technology by police forces in recent years has naturally led to more opportunities for employment in the departments concerned. Computers are in use in several key areas, ranging from administration and such routine matters as police salaries and accounts, to sophisticated traffic management systems and, of course, the Police National Computer at Hendon. Here it should be borne in mind that the Metropolitan Police recruits its civil staff as members of the Civil Service, and because the Force is not subject to the control of local authorities, it has to provide the whole range of ancillary services, whereas provincial police forces in many cases will make use of local government departments to provide some services, such as finance, catering, and so on. In the provinces, some forces recruit their civilian staffs directly and such employees are employed by the Chief Constable. This happens in the case of combined police forces, that is, police forces which cover several county council areas. In the provincial Metropolitan forces which are controlled by the Metropolitan Councils, the employer is the local authority. This has advantages and disadvantages for the employee. If he or she works for the local authority rather than the police force, through the Chief Constable, he is more likely to be able to transfer in and out of the various local government departments. In the combined and Metropolitan forces, civilian employees have to make their careers within the more limited structure which is offered to them.

Police operations

Another area of police operations which now often offers great scope for civilian employment is the operations rooms of the police forces; the 'nerve centres' which receive all incoming communications and send out information and instructions to the officers maintaining police cover round the clock, every day of the year. Communication is nowadays widely dependent on radio links, and nearly all control room staffs include civilian radio operators.

Traffic wardens

By far the most well known and widely seen civilian aids to the

Civilians in the police

police forces are the Traffic Wardens to be seen in nearly every city and small town in the country. They share some characteristics with the police; they are a uniformed and disciplined service in daily and close contact with the public. The work that they perform is vital if the relatively free flow of traffic is to be maintained in city streets which are often under heavy pressure from the volume of traffic. When the Traffic Wardens began to appear on the streets in the early sixties, it was because police officers were having to be used more or less constantly to deal with the problems of on-street parking and obstruction. In addition, when a police officer reported a motorist for a parking offence, he almost always had to appear in court to give evidence against the offender, who never bothered to turn up. So the courts were becoming bogged down with motoring cases and literally hordes of police officers were spending hours on end, waiting in courtrooms to give evidence in these trivial cases. When the law was changed to allow motorists to 'plead guilty' by post, the way was opened for Traffic Wardens to take over this onerous, time consuming and unpopular duty from the police.

Although the work which Traffic Wardens have been allowed to do has been increased slightly, they can now deal with vehicle excise licence offences and direct moving traffic, their work remains inherently unpopular with the motoring public. The motorist, as a breed, is a peculiarly selfish animal. He wants to be able to drive his car up and down the streets with the minimum of inconvenience, and certainly unimpeded by badly parked cars belonging to other motorists. Far from giving the Traffic Warden the credit for maintaining a relatively obstruction free city centre, the motorist will insist on parking where he wants to, for as long as he wishes. When he returns to his car to find a Traffic Warden in the act of giving him a fixed penalty parking notice, invariably he feels resentment or worse. It is a sad truth that Traffic Wardens are frequently assaulted by irate motorists. It is not surprising that all over the country, Traffic Wardens' departments find the greatest difficulty in attracting and retaining the right kind of staff to take on a job which requires considerable tact and patience, and gets more hostility from the general public than it deserves.

Special Constables

Every police force has a corps of unpaid volunteers, called the Special Constabulary. The men and women who belong to this body act as a reserve force, the idea being that in times of local or national emergency, the regular police can be reinforced by them. In the two major wars of this century, Special Constables, played a vital role in maintaining the rule of law. They were needed then to replace regular police officers who were serving in the armed forces. The other most notable occasion when the Special Constabulary was mobilised fully, was the General Strike of 1926, when the Specials assisted their regular colleagues in protecting property and ensuring the movement of essential services.

The Special Constables like to claim that their ancestry goes back hundreds of years beyond the establishment of a professional police force, because they are the modern day equivalent of the ordinary citizens who were deputed to take on the job of the local constable in the hamlets and villages of England. This tradition of citizen involvement in the maintenance of the Sovereign's peace goes back to Saxon times at least.

Today, the Special Constabulary sees its role as providing much needed support for the hard pressed regular police. It has to be said, however, that regular police officers have not always appreciated the work of the Specials. This, on reflection, is understandable. Regular police officers take a great pride in their professionalism, and they do not take kindly to the idea that 'amateurs' can do their work. In the not too distant past, animosity arose between the regular police and the Specials because some police forces used their volunteers in such a way as to avoid the need for employing sufficient numbers of regular police. Forces with holiday resorts in their areas, for example, relied too much on the voluntary assistance of Specials to cope with traffic and crowd problems, presumably because they saw no need to employ more regulars, who would have less work to do in the rest of the year.

Official policy towards the Special Constabulary is intended to allay any anxieties that the regular police might have on this score. The number of regular police officers which each force may have is

Special Constables

not calculated according to the size of the Special Constabulary in that force. Specials must not be used instead of regulars, they are there to complement the professional force. On average, Specials are not expected to perform more than four hours duty each week, and most of their duty periods are devoted to training. The duties they perform are allocated with the purpose of the Special Constabulary in mind; to be an efficient reserve force to come to the aid of the police in times of emergency. So Specials are employed, for the most part, on street patrols and helping with crowd control at public events such as processions, football matches, Royal visits, and so on.

Special Constables have just the same powers at law as have their regular colleagues. They take the same Oath of Allegiance and hold the ancient office of Constable. All the same, because police work is now so complex, they cannot be expected to possess the experience and the expertise which the public expects of its regular police force.

All over the country, there are thousands of men and women who have chosen to serve their communities as Special Constables and, generally speaking, they enjoy very friendly relations with the regular police. Voluntary service as a Special Constable can be very satisfying and rewarding, but the police forces definitely are not looking for officious or authoritative types who want to wear police uniforms and 'push people around'. Now that police forces have far fewer vacancies for regular recruits, most suggest to applicants to whom they are unable to offer a place that the Specials ought to be considered. Some young people join the Specials in the hope that this will increase their chances of eventually becoming regular police officers, but this is not a course to be recommended. The ideal Special is someone who wants to perform community service in his spare time.

Facing the future

The dramatic events of the nineteen eighties have shown the extent of the revolution which is taking place inside the police service, and how the nature of relations between the police and the people has been undergoing major changes.

The most obvious example of rapid change, brought about by the need of the police to respond swiftly to new challenges to the rule of law, concerns public order. The first serious outbreak of rioting occurred in the St Paul's area of Bristol in 1981. The police were taken completely by surprise. Although reinforcements were soon brought in from other forces, there was considerable criticism of the police strategy, particularly the decision to withdraw from the area and leave the rioters, if only for a few hours, virtually in control of the neighbourhood. Police chiefs and politicians were surprised at the clear indication from the St Paul's riot, that the forces of law and order were dangerously thin in the areas which, like St Paul's, were most likely to explode into sudden outbreaks of this kind. The police seemed to have no strategy for quickly restoring their authority when such riots broke out. They had none of the equipment which, in foreign police forces, has always been available to help the police to suppress riots and protect police officers from personal injuries.

When the riots came back to Britain in the following summer of 1981, the police were better prepared, although still not organised sufficiently well to cope with outbreaks on the scale of those which occurred in Southall, Brixton and Toxteth. The result was that there was extensive damage to property and serious injuries on both sides, before the situation in these areas was brought under police control.

Looking back, it is now clear that 1981 marked a watershed in the development of modern policing in Britain. This was the year when it became very plain that, with the possible exception of the Metropolitan Police, no single force is able to contain, from its own resources, a sustained threat to public order, whether that threat comes from street rioters or is part of a national industrial dispute, or a politically motivated campaign. Examples of the latter

Facing the future

two causes of disorder have been the miners' dispute of 1984, involving mass picketing and violence at pitheads, coke depots, ports and power stations all over the country, and the political violence which has been going on in Northern Ireland since 1969. The former was dealt with by the widespread mobilisation of special police units from other forces, and in Ulster the British Army has shored up the hard pressed Royal Ulster Constabulary since the trouble commenced.

The street riots have had two far reaching consequences for the British police. After insisting for more than 150 years that the traditional methods of persuasion and consent were sufficient to keep order, police chiefs and police sentiment, as shared by the rank and file, came almost immediately to the view that these principles were no longer enough. Every force was required to organise, train and equip 'Police Support Units' consisting of male officers who, as and when required, can be mobilised instantly, issued with riot equipment, and dispatched in their own unit transport to the scene of an emergency, either in their own force or anywhere else in the country that they may be needed.

The Police Support Units, or PSUs, are not, strictly speaking, the result of the 1981 riots. It was the miners' strikes of 1972 and 1974, coupled with other national industrial disputes in which mass picketing and violence occurred, which warned the authorities that the police would need to have a more organised response to serious public unrest, but the threat was thought then to be more distant. This led in turn to the setting up of the first PSUs, and to the training of large numbers of police officers in methods of crowd control, using riot shields. However, one of the obvious lessons of 1981 was that these preparations had been overtaken by events. The PSUs which went to the aid of the Merseyside Police force varied from the well equipped and self contained units envisaged in the plans drawn up by the Association of Chief Police Officers (which were presented to the Home Secretary in 1981), to somewhat makeshift teams which actually arrived in Liverpool at the height of the riots without suitable transport and equipment.

Other painful experiences of the 1981 riots were the lack of organisation, understanding of tactics, different concepts of riot control between forces, and communication problems caused by radio equipment that was incompatible with Merseyside's communications systems. Toxteth was the first occasion when the

Facing the future

police were required to put the chief officers' contingency plans to the test. It soon became obvious that there were many lessons to be learned. Here were PSUs from forces all over the country. Men who had never heard of a place called Toxteth found themselves thrown into the battle late at night after, in some cases, having travelled all day from the south of England. They were 'in the dark' in all ways; their briefing was poor and their knowledge of local geography and the situation between the police and the local community non-existent. It became clear that the PSUs lost their effectiveness when trying to work with similar groups from other forces, because of divided leadership and lack of clear objectives. But the lessons were learned. When the miners' strike of 1984 began, with mass picketing of pits still working in Nottinghamshire and other parts of the Midlands, the police response to public disorder had come a long way since Toxteth.

So, the first consequence of the changing public order problems in contemporary Britain, has been the increasing reliance placed by the police on the concept of mutual aid between forces. For the first time ever, the police operations during the coal dispute involved several thousand officers being transported to, and billeted in, the troubled areas. It was demonstrated also that the service was capable of sustaining such a major effort, not just for the limited outbursts experienced during the earlier riots, but over a long drawn out period. Of course, an enormous cost was involved. This, and the fact that chief officers of the police forces acted without seeking authority from their local police authorities, added point to the major debate about the accountability and control of police forces. Local police committees in some areas (all Labour controlled) protested about the activities of the National Reporting Centre. This is part of the police strategy for dealing with major incidents such as strikes. The National Reporting Centre is not a permanent body. It can be set up at New Scotland Yard as and when required; the visit of the Pope to Britain in 1982, the miners' dispute of 1984. Its role is to receive intelligence and co-ordinate information in order to assess when and where police forces require either to receive or to send mutual aid to and from each other.

So far, therefore, although these developments have been rapid, and by British standards revolutionary, the British police service remains a long way from imitating the examples of police forces on the continent. There is nothing in Britain to compare with the

Facing the future

permanent CRS, the 30,000 strong heavily armed and paramilitary anti-riot and security police force set up in France after the war, and so feared by many French citizens. Yet we must remember that senior police officers were saying in 1984 that, whatever critics of the police said about the PSUs, mutual aid, and the National Reporting Centre, the only alternative facing the police, if they were to respond to major challenges to the rule of law, was to set up such a permanent force. That would, of course, be the end of the British police tradition altogether. When the tumult of a coal strike dies away, the PSUs stand down and their members resume normal police duty.

That police tradition may be under threat from the second major consequence of recent developments in the public order field; the acquisition by the police of riot equipment. It has been accepted as a regrettable but unavoidable response to the scale of police casualties in the 1980 and 1981 riots, that the police should have physical protection. This consists of a riot helmet with a visor; protection for vital parts of the body, flame proof overalls, and riot shields. More controversial has been the decision of the Home Secretary to allow police forces to acquire stocks of the 'plastic bullets' which have frequently been used by the police and the army during riots in Northern Ireland. Their use in Ulster has been criticised, and a number of deaths have resulted. The security forces retort that since plastic bullets, or baton rounds (to give them their correct title) have been used, the number of casualties sustained by the security forces during riots has been reduced considerably. It is this experience, and the fact that the use of baton rounds has been effective in deterring would-be rioters, that has influenced the police forces on the mainland of Britain. Although the authority to police forces was given in 1982, at the time of writing (mid 1984) there had been no question of their being used by a mainland police force. This has not prevented bitter arguments between Chief Constables and police authorities who are emotionally opposed to the idea of baton rounds with all their Northern Ireland connotations being used in their police forces. Just as the single example of British police firing tear gas at rioters, which occurred at the height of the Toxteth riots, caused a major political row, so would the first use of baton rounds lead to a strong reaction from those who believe that a stronger police response to public order will, indeed, undermine the tradition of

Facing the future

policing by consent on which the British police have so far relied.

Public order is just one of the many major problems which appears to be taking on much greater dimensions during the 1980s. Not the least of these is drug abuse which has taken on alarming proportions in very recent years. Clear evidence has emerged of widespread use, not simply of the relatively milder drugs such as marijuana, but of halucinatory drugs and, worst of all, heroin. In inner city areas in particular, there is a fear that unemployed youngsters are turning to crime as their only means of obtaining heroin. Unemployment and the growing sense of hopelessness of young people in areas where job prospects are minimal, is already leading to major increases in crime levels in our largest cities.

The police can therefore expect to be called upon to meet many major challenges in the immediate future. The service appears to be in the midst of a critical phase when it has to establish its ability to contain the major challenge of crime on the streets whilst retaining the goodwill it already possesses from the majority of the public, and making genuine efforts to establish an improved relationship with young people and ethnic minorities, where relationships have never been as good as with the population in general.

To meet these challenges, the police service is going through yet another period of rapid reorganisation and internal reappraisal of its objectives. The emphasis now is very much on efficiency and 'value for money'. A police officer has become a very expensive commodity in terms of pay and other expenses. More and more 'civilians' are likely to be recruited to ensure that police officers are used only on duties which require police powers or police experience and expertise. There has been a major upsurge in the size of police forces since the mid 1970s, but financial restraints mean that this expansion is unlikely to go on. For the prospective police recruit this means that opportunities to join the service are more limited than they were, and the young men and women anxious for police careers will find police forces being very selective indeed.

In spite of all the problems of our modern society and the near to impossible task which is placed upon the shoulders of every police officer, this still remains one of the most worthwhile, rewarding and fascinating of all careers.

Index

Alderson, John   65, 66, 104
Anderton, James   101
Anti-Terrorist branch   50
Arbuthnot, Jane   74
Assistant Chief Constable *(and Leadership)*   94
Astor, Lady   70
Atomic Energy Authority Police   125
Avon & Somerset   23

Bailey, Stanley   101
Beats   25, 58, 60, 63
Breathalyser   103
Brixton riots   9, 10, 11, 12, 34, 66, 68, 115—6
Buckingham Palace   60

Camps, Professor Francis   127
Career prospects   58
Chief Constables *(and Leadership)*   99—115
Chief Inspector   88
Chief Superintendent *(and Leadership)*   91—94
Civilians   127—131
Codes of (Police) Practice   110, 112
Commander (Metropolitan Police)   25, 72
Commissioner of Police   25, 72, 100, 103, 115
Community policing   65—68
Computers   130
Crime prevention   53
Criminal Investigation Department   25, 43—50
Crown prosecuter   103
CRS (France)   11, 137

Daily Mail   108

Deputy Chief Constable *(and Leadership)*   96—99
Derbyshire Police   102
Detective Superintendent *(and Leadership)*   88
Detective Training School   89
Detention powers   111
Devon & Cornwall   23, 65, 104
Director of Public Prosecutions   91
Discipline (Police)   20, 113—4
Divisional Commanders   91—4
Docks Police   125
Drugs   136

Edmund Davies, Lord   21
Equal Pay Act   69—70

Family lives (of police)   18
Fingerprints   127
Fletcher, Yvonne   77
Forensic Science   51
French police   11

Gilbert, W A   16, 91
Graduate entry   40
Gregory, Ronald   101

Handsworth   66
Helicopter Units   123
Home Beat officers   63
Home Secretary   23, 106, 108, 115
Horwood, General   70

Initial training   30
Inspector *(and Leadership)*   85—88
Inspector of Constabulary   24, 102, 117

139

Index

Interpol 50
IRA 50
Iranian Embassy 51

King, John 106
Knight, Ted 68

Labour Party 118—9, 136
Leadership 78—105

Macready, General Sir Nevil 70
Magna Carta 106
Manchester, Greater 23, 24, 101, 119
Mark, Sir Robert 106
Martin, Maureen 74
McNee, Sir David 105, 109
Merseyside 23, 72, 101, 119, 135
Metropolitan forces (provincial) 23
Metropolitan Police 12, 15, 23, 25, 30, 39, 72, 74, 115, 134
Military Police 125
Ministry of Defence Police 124
'Mods' (and 'Rockers') 10
Moss Side riots 102, 119
Mountain Rescue Teams 121—22
Murder cases 48
Murders (of police) 19, 101

National Front 35
National Reporting Centre 136
Neighbourhood constables 64
Northern Ireland 9, 19, 81, 106, 137
Northumberland Police 101
Nottingham City Police 117
Nottinghamshire 94

Oath of office 112
Organised crime 48
Oxford, Kenneth 101

Pathologists 49, 127
Peace-keeping 51
Peel, Sir Robert 79
Plastic bullets 137

Police accountability 114—119
Police Act 1964 102, 116—118
Police Advisory Board 117
Police authorities 23, 116, 119
Police cadets 26, 36
Police corruption 12
Police and Criminal Evidence Act 44, 104, 106
Police dogs 120—21
Police Federation 71, 79
Police horses 122
Police housing 21
Police Negotiating Board 117
Police pay 21
Police pensions 21
Police perjury 46
Police photographers 129
Police Powers 106—119
Police Staff College 39, 40, 41, 79, 86, 88
Police Support Units 135
Policy Studies Institute 72, 74, 76
Police training 30—32
Probation period 29, 35
Procurator Fiscal 103
Promotion 39, 41
'Punks' 10

Qualifications (for police) 15, 27
Questioning 45

Race relations 34, 35, 36
Ranks in the police 79
Rastafarians 34
Regional Crime Squads 49
Retirement ages 57
Richardson, Superintendent Gerald I, GC 13, 14
Riots 9
River Police 122
Road Safety Act 102
Royal Commission on Criminal Procedure (1978—81) 108—110
Royal Commission (1929) 70

140

Index

Royal Commission (1960—62) 107
Royal Parks Police 125
Royal Ulster Constabulary 42, 99, 101, 124

Salisbury, Bishop of 77
Salmon, Lord 108
Scarman, Lord 9, 11, 19, 29, 35, 61, 103, 115
Scenes of Crime Officers 51, 128
Scotland 24, 99
Scotland Yard 70, 92, 127, 136
Sergeant *(and Leadership)* 82—86
Sex Discrimination Act 69, 71, 72
Shift systems 25
'Skins' 10
Southall riots 134
South Yorkshire 23
Special Branch 50, 51, 119
Special Constables 132—33
Special Course 40, 88
Special Patrol Group 119
Spilsbury, Sir Bernard 127
St Paul's (Bristol) 134
Stolen motor vehicles 50

Stop and Search powers 109—10
Sun, The 108
Sussex 102

Tear Gas 119, 137
Terrorism 50, 106
Thames Valley 123
Towers, Liddle 101
Toxteth riots 10, 12, 66, 101, 119, 134—36
Traffic Departments 54—6
Traffic Wardens 130
Training 30, 33
Transport Police 124
Trenchard, Lord 39
Truman, President 99
Tutor constables 31, 32, 33

Underwater search units 121
Uniformed police 57—68

West Indians 34, 35
West Mercia 23
West Midlands 23, 24, 80, 119
West Yorkshire 23, 101, 118
Wiltshire 23
Women police 69—77

'Yorkshire Ripper' 49, 101, 118